FOR THE KING'S SERVICE
RAILWAY SHIPS AT WAR

A. J. Mullay

PENDRAGON

"His Majesty's Government relies on the goodwill of yourselves, your staff and agents, in carrying out these instructions and preparing the ship for the King's service"
Ministry of Shipping letter to Railway Company Managers, 1940.

The Scotia *was one of four vessels requisitioned from the LNWR in August 1914.*
Two of her sisters were lost in the conflict.

All photographs are from the
J. & C. McCutcheon Collection
unless otherwise indicated.

FOR THE KING'S SERVICE
RAILWAY SHIPS
AT WAR
A. J. Mullay

PENDRAGON

The LNER's Talisman *saw service in World War Two as* HMS Aristocrat.
She returned to civilian life with the LNER and later with BR, as seen here, until 1967.

Published by Pendragon Publishing, PO Box 3, Easingwold, York, YO61 3YS.

Design by Barry C. Lane, Sutton-in-Craven, West Yorkshire

Printed by The Amadeus Press, Cleckheaton, West Yorkshire

British Cataloguing-in-Publication Data: a catalogue reference for this book is held by the British Library.

ISBN No.978 1 899816 16 3

CONTENTS

Chapter 1
INTRODUCTION

Ferry services around the British coast were once described by the Chairman of the British Transport Commission (BTC) as "a projection of the railway system across the narrow seas". This is a succinct summing-up of a transport network vastly different from the present day, but which served the public travelling between Britain and the Continent, and Britain and Ireland – as well as the Channel Islands, Western Isles and the Isles of Scilly – for around 120 years.

Ferries, cargo boats, dredgers, tugs, all these were owned by up to twenty railways at various times and that does not include pleasure steamers on lake, loch and estuary. One of the latter – the *Waverley* – is still cruising today and it takes an effort of imagination to envisage a flotilla of paddle steamers, their bright colours over-painted with grey, forming a mine-sweeping patrol; yet this happened as recently as World War Two. But the near-absence of Sealink ships, once owned by the nationalised rail network, to find their way to the Falklands during the 1982 conflict (only one was present) is an indication of how railways have lost their predominant place in inshore passenger sailing.

The real story of ferries and pleasure vessels at war came in World Wars One and Two. Railway-owned ships found themselves tussling with U-boats, supporting the Gallipoli landings, searching for the German High Seas Fleet at Jutland, evacuating troops at Dunkirk and landing them again on D-Day. Railway ship crews were killed by explosions, drownings and, in one case, shot by German firing-squad, while others were taken prisoner, interned even before war was declared and, in one notorious case, forced-marched through the Sahara Desert by hostile nomadic tribesmen. As if that were not enough, only in the final year of World War One was it decided that these railwaymen-at-sea should be paid the same as other seamen. For most of that war, this was a workforce that was underpaid as well as mortally endangered. In both wars, their contributions to victory were barely mentioned in the official histories commissioned by Government.

Their story is one of courage and defiance. While it requires fortitude to face the enemy when sailing in an armoured warship, or surrounded by fellow servicemen

armed and ready for action, it takes twice as much when serving in a civilian ship whose thin-skinned hull could be penetrated by a torpedo or mine at any time, and whose fellow crew-members were unarmed and untrained in combat. If railwaymen and women showed courage in facing attacks on land from airship and bomber, this was even more evident at sea, facing submarine and commerce raider as well. This book is dedicated to their memory.

Naval craft are expected to operate in all weather conditions and in the face of enemy aggression, so a high turnover of military vessels was inevitable in any conflict from the Napoleonic Wars to Operation Corporate to recapture the Falklands in 1982. Equally, many varieties of civilian vessel, particularly liners, pleasure steamers and ferries, would find their normal duties interrupted and even cancelled in war conditions, effectively making them available for emergency duties. This was not invariably the case and there were notable exceptions where ferry routes were maintained by the railway companies even in a war zone – the Great Eastern's continued operation of the Harwich–Hook of Holland service in World War One is a good example. Indeed, this particular company had to *increase* its service on this route, in the teeth of U-boat attacks, chartering from other railways in doing so. The Royal Navy's failure to protect these sailings was a continuing problem, culminating in farce in the autumn of 1916, as will be revealed.

In two World Wars, there was no question of civilian steamers being tied up in port "for the duration". On the contrary, displaced railway steamers were very much to the fore as they swept mines, evacuated troops from retreat, landed troops in attack and faced up to U-Boats. Unfortunately, the U-boats usually won these unequal battles against unarmed, or lightly armed, railway ships.

But not always. The Great Eastern Railway-owned steamer *Brussels* attempted to ram a U-Boat in 1915, an action for which her captain was later executed (ie murdered) by the Germans and there were other clashes between steamers and submarine. The North Eastern's *Kirkham Abbey,* for example, met the enemy twice before her final sinking by torpedo, on one occasion using her speed to outpace a surfaced submarine.

At the outbreak of World War One on 4th August 1914, the Royal Navy had no auxiliary minesweepers; by the end of the war it had 156 on its strength. Not until late in the war could minesweeping be undertaken by one ship at a time; earlier methods involved two vessels towing trawl gear behind them, thus doubling the risk to the sweeping craft. In the first two months of World War One, one sweeping vessel (initially, a trawler) was being lost for every two mines swept, although this alarming ratio had settled down at 1:80 by the end of the war. The requisitioned ships lost in the years 1914-18 came to over 800, although that included other auxiliary categories such as hospital ships.

At this point it should be explained that a 'hospital ship' – a category of vessel which figured prominently in both World Wars – was effectively an ambulance carrier and not a floating hospital where anything other than rudimentary medical treatment was given. Nevertheless, not until 1918 was the description 'hospital ship' changed, so it is so rendered in this history of railway ships in World War One, especially as the listing continued in the Official History of the war at sea first published in 1921 (see Bibliography under 'Corbett').

Railway companies' marine losses ran at around 25% of their fleet complements, although that fails to take into account the state in which many surviving vessels were returned to their owners. Some, like the afore-mentioned *Brussels* of the Great Eastern, had already been to the bottom and raised again (and this particular vessel was not taken back). Others, such as the three Great Central Railway ships impounded by the Germans (probably illegally) in August 1914 had been denied to their owning company, or to naval service, for the entire war, and their crews effectively prisoners-of-war from the very day it began.

The official figures amount to nearly one thousand vessels available for the Navy to take up from trade in 1914, since most shipyard capacity was occupied by warship construction. In other words, railway vessels, released from pleasure cruising and ferry duties, provided a vital source of fleet auxiliaries, but represented a non-renewable resource, one which was running down with every new year of war. No shipyard would build a civilian ferry when a minesweeper could be constructed in the same time; even repair facilities were often unavailable to the companies. The railway ships were not only vital to the war effort, they were literally irreplaceable.

Great Eastern Railway Archangel *with prisoners of war, November 1918*

Despite being named for a holiday resort associated with a playboy lifestyle, the Biarritz *of the SECR and later Southern Railway, could boast a distinguished fighting record in two world wars. In the first she proved to be a prolific minelayer in both home and Mediterranean waters, despite her deadly ordnance having to be stored on the upper deck, threatening her stability. She is seen here (above) in 1917 at Mudros in the Mediterranean, where she was credited with the destruction of a German cruiser and the crippling of a battlecruiser. The launch rails for mines are hidden by canvas screens at the stern. Below she is seen at Folkestone in happier times, sailing for her Southern Railway owners.*

Chapter 2
THE RAILWAY SHIP OWNERS
AND WHERE THEY OPERATED

Railway operators in Britain before World Wars One and Two will be summarised here, if only to explain why what would appear to be exclusively terrestrial transport concerns had maritime resources so attractive to the naval authorities. In fact, as will be shown later, the legislation enabling railway vessels to be commandeered to support military operations failed to mention ships, merely 'plant', but nearly every major railway – certainly eleven out of the largest twelve – operated ships as a matter of course by 1914. (See Tables I and II).

Historically, railways were not the first transport companies to be formed to operate in Britain – canals could claim that title – but they were the largest. When the London Midland & Scottish Railway was formed in 1923 from such giants in their own right as the London & North Western and the Midland, it was nearly 50 times the size of the largest steel company, with a workforce to equal the peacetime British Army in numbers. In 1940 the LMS president, Lord Stamp, was asked by Prime Minister Neville Chamberlain to undertake the post of Chancellor of the Exchequer, but turned it down on the advice of the Governor of the Bank of England, presumably because running the LMS was job enough. The company's creation followed an enforced amalgamation of companies known as the 'Grouping' established by the 1921 Transport Act, but this brief survey of the companies begins in 1914 when the companies were still independent, and almost invariably prosperous, with their takeover by the Government-imposed Railway Executive Committee seen as a matter of national necessity at a time of international turmoil.

This brief survey of railway-owned coastal shipping takes a clockwise direction on the map of mainland Britain, beginning in North East England, coincidentally the matrix for railway development in the first place. This area was effectively monopolised by one company, the North Eastern Railway, based in York but running services in and around the river mouths of Tweed, Tyne, Wear, Tees and Humber. By the time Britain's railways were grouped in 1923, the NER had consolidated its influence southwards, taking over the Hull & Barnsley

Railway in 1922. This considerably increased the mercantile interests of a company whose seaborne existence had previously consisted of little more than harbour craft such as tugs and dredgers, with the Scandinavian and Baltic trade largely left in the hands of associated shipping companies. The NER's interest in these meant that it did not itself exercise its trading rights out of Hull, nor was it active out of Newcastle. By 1923, the rail company had been associated with Thomas Wilson and Co. of Hull, as well as the Hull & Netherlands Steamship Company. Some of their ships are treated as 'railway' vessels for the purpose of this narrative, with (in the Wilson case) a distinctive joint funnel livery comprising a white band in between the previous Wilson colours of red with a black top.

On the south side of the Humber, two railway companies looked seawards for revenue. Operating out of Goole was the Lancashire & Yorkshire which, like the Hull & Barnsley, was to lose its existence shortly before the Grouping took place, amalgamating with the London & North Western. The 'Lanky' was no small player in the world of coastal shipping, sailing from Fleetwood on the west as well as Goole and Hull on the east, and taking a terrible pounding in World War One. One author calculates that nearly a quarter of all naval requisitions from rail companies in World War One came from this comparatively minor railway.

Also heavily involved in shipping out of Goole (as well as Grimsby, Immingham, and New Holland) was the Great Central Railway, a regional company operating across England between Manchester and the East Coast. Originally named the Manchester, Sheffield & Lincolnshire, this railway was ambitious enough to build the last main line south to London, even when it duplicated three existing routes. Although trading with Belgium, the Baltic was this company's prime traffic area, including such German ports as Hamburg, thus ensuring that the GCR would be affected by war as soon as the first shot was fired. Even earlier in fact, with three of the company's ships interned by the Germans before war was actually declared. This curious incident, one which must have been distressing for the crews and their

Exhibiting all the confidence and elegance of the Edwardian decade, the Midland Railway's Antrim *was introduced on the Heysham–Belfast passage in 1904. She was a 2,000-tonner capable of 20 knots, but had a comparatively quiet war before being sold to the Isle of Man SP Company in 1928. Her near-sister* Donegal *was less lucky, being sunk by torpedo in the English Channel in April 1917 while working as a hospital ship.*

loved ones at home, is discussed later. At least the crewmen did not face the very real possibility of being mined or torpedoed. Apart from the loss of these three ships seized by the enemy, the Great Central was to lose one operational ship in four.

Moving southwards down the east coast, we come to the Great Eastern Railway, headquartered at London's Liverpool Street and spreading deep through Essex and into Norfolk and Suffolk. In the first-named county, the port of Harwich was central to this company's operations, so central in fact that the GER constructed the principal harbour facility here, Parkeston Quay, opened in 1883. Named for the company chairman, this terminal facilitated the transfer of passenger and goods between train and ship. The Great Eastern Railway was noteworthy for maintaining – and increasing – its

The Great Central Railway was unlucky in having three of its ships in German waters in August 1914 and none managed to escape, all being interned at Hamburg, with their railway crews sent to Ruhleben, a racecourse turned into an internment camp near Berlin. This shot shows City of Leeds – *she survived 'imprisonment' but, unlike some of her sisters, was unable to make up for it in the next war, being withdrawn in 1937.*

existing services to and from the Netherlands in World War One despite the inherent dangers involved; indeed, a number of the confrontations between railway vessel and U-boat in the early part of the war involved ships still sailing the company flag and in no way considered naval vessels. By the end of the conflict, the GER had trebled the number of ships working the Harwich–Hook of Holland route, chartering from the Great Central in order to maintain services, even though Parkeston Quay was not always available. Some of the most stirring tales of bravery concern Great Eastern captains and crew, two of the skippers involved being decorated after successfully counter-attacking and scaring off U-boats.

South of the Thames, the Kent coast sailings were monopolised by the South Eastern & Chatham Railway from 1899 until the Grouping. It ran services in and out of the important ports of Dover and Folkestone, with seven turbine-powered vessels responsible for this crucial passage, made ever more important by wartime traffic. In 1910 the company's trains and ships could deposit a Paris-bound passenger on French soil four hours after leaving London, with an overall advertised journey time to Paris of less than seven hours – faster than travelling from London to Edinburgh at that time. While the railway suffered ship losses like any other 'line', it was the naval deployment of two of its vessels that was truly remarkable. One made an important intervention in the Battle of Jutland in 1916, while another laid mines which destroyed or crippled two German capital ships in World War One and survived shelling at Dunkirk in the second conflict.

The Great Central operated a number of freighters, most of them redundant during war as German ports were their usual destination. Two introduced just before World War One were the Chesterfield *and the* Macclesfield. *This shot shows detail of the stern one of the Tyne-built sisters.*

Like City of Leeds, *the Great Central's* Bury *was interned at* Hamburg *in the first world conflict, but made for this in the second, acting as a rescue ship during the Battle of the Atlantic from 1941. In May of the following year she picked up so many survivors from sinking merchant ships that she was in danger of running out of food. She resumed commercial service until 1958 – not a bad record for a vessel deemed useful only for sinking as a blockship in 1940 in a plan to close Blyth harbour against an invader!*

The next company to be encountered in this clockwise coverage of Britain's coasts was the London Brighton & South Coast, sailing between Newhaven and Dieppe on what its advertisements called the 'Royal Mail Route to Paris and the Continent'. It shared Isle of Wight sailings out of Portsmouth with the London & South Western Railway, itself busy with Channel Islands traffic through Southampton, whence services were also run to Le Havre, Cherbourg and St. Malo. It was in fact this latter railway, and its Southampton harbour, that was to bear the brunt of conveying the British Expeditionary Force to France in 1914. At one time a train was arriving at the quayside every twelve minutes – and this over a fourteen-hour period.

No 4. Zeebrugge
Hull Boat Duke of Clarence.

The Lancashire & Yorkshire Railway was very active in maritime matters, operating on east and west coasts. After completion in 1892, the Duke of Clarence *plied out of Fleetwood, but in Edwardian times spent most of the year sailing between Hull and Zeebrugge. She survived nearly four years of war service, lasting until 1930.*

Pride of the London & North Western Railway fleet were the four packet ships for the Holyhead–Dublin service, named for the (then) four nations of the United Kingdom. In this commercial postcard, TSS Anglia *is seen on passage in the Irish Sea. Unfortunately, she was mined with great loss of life in November 1915, within a mile of Folkestone harbour, not long after taking King George V across the Channel.*

The North Eastern Railway took a financial interest in the Hull & Netherlands Company in 1908 and this was one of four sister vessels introduced around that time. This is Whitby Abbey, *a WWI survivor having been requisitioned for nearly four years, at a time when a number of NE-based ships fell foul of the enemy.*

The Great Eastern Railway operated across the North Sea to the Hook of Holland and her ship masters found themselves confronted by German U-Boats on a number of occasions. Advice given them by the Admiralty was almost suicidal if put into practice and one ship's master who incurred German wrath was the captain of the Brussels. *She was captured in 1916 and her master Captain Fryatt put to death. After the ship had been sunk and recovered, she became the* Lady Brussels, *plying the Irish Sea.*

The Great Western Railway was criticised by maritime historians Duckworth and Langmuir for the 'ugliness' of the company's ship funnels, in contrast to the copper-capped chimneys of Swindon-built locomotives. Whether justified or not, GWR ships made a major contribution in both world wars, but the Ibex, *dating from 1891, operated on the Weymouth– Channel Islands service during WWI while three company vessels were requisitioned for minelaying.* Ibex *survived a sinking in 1900 and is reported to have fought off a U-Boat during the war.*

Next was the Great Western, considered by many as the UK's leading railway, and which was to be comparatively unchanged by the 1923 Grouping. Not only prominent on land, the GWR was an active ship operator on no fewer than three coasts in England and Wales. This company was to lose the first railway steamer to be sunk in World War One, although not in the Great Western's usual ambit. On the south coast, GWR steamers connected Weymouth with the Channel Islands, while Ireland was the destination from Fishguard on the south west coast of Wales.

North westwards, we come to the packet station of Holyhead, whence LNWR steamers plied to Ireland, particularly Dublin. Services to the north of Ireland were more commonly operated by the company from Fleetwood, taking over the former LYR's commitments. North of here there were services to Ireland and the Isle of Man by the Midland Railway operating out of Heysham, near Morecambe. This company also had a share in the steamship company running the Stranraer–Larne crossing, jointly with the LNWR, Caledonian and Glasgow & South Western.

The smallest railway operating shipping was the Furness. Based at Barrow, it ran pleasure sailings down the coast to Fleetwood, but its paddle steamers *Lady Evelyn* and *Lady Moyra* also plied to and from the Isle of

One of the most elegant fleets of railway ships comprised those operated by the South Eastern & Chatham Railway across the English Channel. This stern shot shows the Riviera *leaving the White Cliffs behind. She survived both world wars, but her wartime appearance was completely different from this, although she was not converted into a primitive aircraft carrier like her sister* Engadine.

Man and Belfast. They brought pleasure to thousands of trippers, but also served in two world wars, the second under non-railway management, and both were sunk, one becoming wrecked, the other bombed by the Luftwaffe when it was evacuating troops from Dunkirk. The Furness also operated a number of tugs, as well as pleasure sailings on Lakes Coniston and Windermere.

The two Glasgow-based Scottish companies were very active on the Clyde coast as might be expected; between them the Caledonian and Glasgow & South Western bequeathed some twenty vessels to the LMS at Grouping. The biggest Scottish company before 1923, the North British, also operated ships on the Clyde and, to a lesser extent, on the Forth and Solway.

Pride of the Caledonian fleet was the turbine-powered steamer, the Duchess of Argyll. *Her owners insured for her three times that of her paddle steamer sisters in the fleet, but she was no diva, undertaking 655 military voyages in the Great War and twice coming to the rescue of ships damaged in the English Channel. She survived both conflicts and was nationalised with her railway owners in 1948.*

As can be seen from the timeline table, the 1921 Transport Act, which came into effect on 1st January 1923, allocated around 120 companies into four large concerns. These were the Great Western (virtually unchanged from before 1923 except for the addition of some Welsh lines) and the Southern, taking in the three companies south of the Thames. But the two other, larger grouped companies were more of a mixed bag. Largest of all was the London Midland & Scottish. As already mentioned this was the biggest company in Britain at the time of its formation, but this narrative will concentrate on the LMS's non-rail activities (which included licence to operate flights as far east as Yugoslavia!). At the height of its maritime operations, the company owned no fewer than 74 steamers, based on the former fleets of the LNWR (including the then newly-absorbed LYR),

Midland, Furness, Caledonian and G&SW. It operated on both East and West Coasts, from Goole on the Humber to Gourock on the Clyde, and including the Lancastrian ports. The LMS was also represented on inland waters such as Coniston, Windermere and Lochs Awe, Etive and Lomond. Among the more famous of the companies in which the LMS had an interest was David MacBrayne's.

The London & North Eastern Railway was almost the equal of the LMS in share value, but had less of a marine presence, being active on the West Coast only in Scotland. Its main centres of maritime activity south of the Border comprised the former Great Central and Great Eastern networks, with a lesser presence in the North East. In Scotland, the company had inherited the marine assets of the North British Railway, losing two

15

The Glasgow & South Western Railway had no inferiority complex when it came to marine matters and this vessel, the Mercury, *was one reason why. Launched in 1892, she could attain 18 knots on the run to the Kyles of Bute and is seen in this 1916 shot in military garb, with her observation lounges panelled over. While minesweeping she survived having her stern blown off, but within one day of returning to duty, had her bow blown off! Perhaps surprisingly, she was able to resume civilian duties after the war and also served the LMS until 1933.*

of that former company's paddle steamers on active service in World War Two. Surprisingly, the LNER immediately set about replacing one of them – and so we can enjoy sailings on the paddle steamer *Waverley,* fourth to bear that name, and charming new generations of pleasure trip customers.

These 'Big Four' companies – GWR, SR, LMS, and LNER – lasted some 25 years before being nationalised by Clement Attlee's Socialist administration on 1st January 1948. An innovation set up at that time was the British Transport Commission – an attempt to integrate all of the British transport industry, with the exception of air travel. Its first head was Sir Cyril (later, Lord)

Hurcomb and he announced that ferry routes would effectively be considered as extensions of the railways. (Vehicle ferries were not in the same demand as nowadays!) For some twenty years, rail managements ran much of Britain's inshore shipping well, and with increased profitability, until the 1968 Transport Act led to the setting up of a section within British Railways called the Ship & International Services Division.

If critics wondered at that time if this was likely to trigger a selling-off of railway ships, they were prescient, with a later Conservative government accomplishing such a sell-off in 1984. But the final assessment of the merits of railway ownership of inshore shipping can be left with historian Michael Bonavia, formerly a senior staff member of the British Transport Commission. Dr. Bonavia points out in one of his books on nationalised railways that "overall, the shipping services never failed to make a profit... railwaymen could look enviously [proudly?] upon this record".

In 1982 the Falklands conflict led to a new demand from civilian ships to supplement and support the Royal Navy. It was a sign of the times that railway vessels played almost no part in this campaign; indeed the Merchant Navy proved unable to meet all the Navy's needs and foreign fleets had to be searched in fulfilling a renewed programme of STUFT.

Chapter 3
THE HISTORY OF STUFT - WORLD WAR ONE

The process of requisitioning civilian ships as and when required by the military is known as STUFT – Ships Taken Up from Trade – and was last put into effect in 1982. But the division between the Merchant and Royal Navies has never been entirely clear-cut anyway. Traditionally, the former has provided the latter with 'hulls in the water' when the demands of War exceeded the existing number of vessels available to sail under, or assist, the White Ensign.

When Captain Cook explored the unknown parts of the southern hemisphere, he did so in a requisitioned Whitby collier. Darwin and Fitzroy sailed to the Galapagos in a former cargo vessel, and Captain Scott set off for the Pole in a converted whaling ship. Although all of these were naval expeditions, the Royal Navy has a tradition of 'horses for courses', and as a result might very well view paddle steamers, with their shallow drafts, as perfect for minesweeping, train ferries' wide decks ideal for minelaying, and pleasure vessels, with generous daytime accommodation, as just what was required for troop-carrying.

Legislation enabling the Government to take ships out of the railways' shipping fleets for military use, reached the Statute Book, not in 1914 with the seemingly all-embracing Defence of the Realm Act, but in August 1871. At that time, with the Franco-Prussian War making London uneasy at the speed of the Germanic victory, a Regulation of the Forces Act was hastily passed. Effectively, this Act allowed the Royal Navy to acquire railway vessels as and when it liked, with no immediate payment taking place. And the Navy was not slow in 1914 to put the STUFT programme into effect.

Clause 16 of this legislation gave the Government the right to take "possession of any railroad in the United Kingdom, and of the plant belonging thereto, and of any part thereof". Ships were not specifically mentioned and in 1871, the rail companies were only just becoming interested in offshore operations, in some cases after encountering legal challenges from existing shipping lines and having to set up "arm's length" companies to

undertake daily maritime services. Confusingly, both the Regulation of the Forces Act and the Regulation of Railways Act were passed within four days of each other in August 1871. The latter did not address the question of military requisition, although it did rule on the compensation arrangements for shipwrecked passengers where a railway company had chartered another company's vessel. In some respects, this nominally addressed the railways' ship ownership more than the Forces Act, which did not mention rail ships, but certainly was taken to have included them by the military authorities in 1914.

By that time, railway ships were simply understood to be, in a way scarcely imaginable nowadays, part and parcel of a major railway company. Of the top dozen railways, only the Great Northern did not operate coastal or ferry shipping, and it is significant that of the 46 railways *not* taken over by the new Railway Executive Committee in 1914, not one operated ships or canals. Incidentally, of those 46 omissions, several were intensively busy underground systems in London and Glasgow, as well as such Welsh bylines likely to be of little interest to the new authority as the Talyllyn and Corris, so traffic turnover, great or small, was obviously not a factor in the Railway Executive Committee's selection process. Curiously, Acting Executive chairman Herbert Walker listed only 36 companies excluded from REC supervision when writing to the Secretary of the Railway Clearing House in August 1914, adding that any lines not listed could be considered to be outside the scheme, but a certain amount of clerical imprecision is evident in the official papers, and a correcting letter had to be sent later. What *is* significant is that any railway company operating so much as a mile of canal, or a single ship, was taken over.

According to Edwin Pratt, historian of Britain's railways in World War One, War Office staff felt that Clause 16 of the 1871 Regulation of the Forces Act was so poorly drawn up as to be a 'dead letter'; in particular, its citing of the 'possession' of railways (or 'railroads' as it called them), could imply a transfer of ownership rather than the (presumably intended) reference to a physical takeover in order to ensure that military purposes were prioritised. Poorly drafted or not, the 1871 Act was seized on by the naval authorities in 1914, as it allowed for immediate railway ship takeovers by Government without any complicated discussion about compensation. Effectively, Mr. Pratt records that "the Admiralty got the railway-owned boats without any payment for them"; indeed the companies were required to fuel, maintain and crew these vessels at their own expense when in naval service, even having to adapt them for Admiralty use. Not surprisingly "certain of the companies protested against these expectations", but these working expenses were recoverable from the Government.

Archival records show that letters went out from the Admiralty to companies on Wednesday 22nd July, under the heading 'Navy War Order System', so it seems that railways were among the first shipowners to 'volunteer' use of their vessels in 1914, on the 'you, you and you' principle. If all this seems too informal to be true, Pratt is keen to emphasise that his two-volume *British railways and the Great War* was written with the co-operation of the pre-Grouping rail companies' senior managers and board members, and there seems no doubt that the 1871 measure was regarded by them as the enabling legislation, even although a later Act of Parliament in 1883 was intended to address this point and 'tidy up' apparent anomalies.

Minesweeping in World War One was undertaken by two vessels dragging trawl gear intended to snag a mine and bring it to the surface for explosion by gunfire. The latter was not always successful and this picture shows a boat crew having to approach a mine in order to attach an explosive charge by hand. The paddle steamer in the background is unidentified, but most railway steamers of this type were requisitioned for this kind of warfare, not only in this war but in the next conflict as well.

The Great Eastern Railway ships were involved in World War One from the first week, with their ferry St. Petersburg *taking the German and British ambassadors across the North Sea to their respective home countries. This ship was later renamed* Archangel *but was targeted successfully by the Luftwaffe in the next war.*

In one of his earliest circular letters from the Railway Executive, in August 1914, Walker assured the companies that the powers invested under Section 16 of the 1871 Regulation of the Forces Act would be enforced and renewed "from week to week as long as the Emergency continues". (In 1916 the Board of Trade gave notice that a post-war period of control would be implemented instead. Incidentally, Walker was always designated as 'Acting Chairman' of the REC, the President of the Board theoretically being Chairman). In any event, the use of the term 'emergency' as opposed to 'World War One' or 'Great War' indicates a belief in 1914, perhaps an almost subconscious one, that the world could be pulled back from this madness, even as German troops marched through Belgium. This is confirmed by another interesting bulletin from Walker which has survived in the public archives.

In September 1914 the Executive's acting chairman circulated all railways expressing concern that the outbreak of war had happened at such a time (early August) that many citizens "were not able to get away for their summer holidays". As a result he sanctioned the companies to extend excursion fare offers beyond 30th September and the Great Northern, in whose files this copy letter was found, immediately announced that a new cut-off date of 30th November would be introduced, so as to allow visitors time and opportunity to travel to "seaside towns and holiday resorts", although not including Scottish or Irish destinations. It is an astonishing bulletin to read, betraying as it does the authorities' lack of awareness of what the experience of total war was going to be like.

This casual attitude misfired horribly in the short term, resulting in rail companies having to operate normal passenger services, including restaurant cars, at the height of summer, while facing unprecedented demands for coaching stock for troop movements, and all this with a suddenly diminishing labour force. As the war went on, the REC's policy encouraged civilians to *expect* continuing holiday arrangements at a time when huge demands were being made on the network in the form of troop specials and entirely new freight traffic streams. In addition, some companies were repeatedly asked to supply locomotives and rolling stock to neighbour companies, or to the armed forces themselves. By the middle of the following April, Walker was distributing guidelines on the free transport of soldiers' and sailors' corpses, the paperwork for which was to be kept well away from the public's eyes. By 1917 excursions fares

The Great Eastern steamer Brussels *was one of the most celebrated, and unfortunate, railway ships operating in World War One. Continuing on her peacetime route between Harwich and the Netherlands, she was captured by the Germans in 1916, her captain then being executed because of a previous incident when the enemy believed Captain Fryatt had abused truce conditions. The ship herself was sunk by the British when in enemy hands at Zeebrugge in October 1918 and is seen here not long after her raising in the following year. She was never to carry passengers again, being converted for livestock transport.*

had to be increased to stop people travelling and around 400 stations closed. Clearly, Walker and his fellow RE Committee members had had no conception of Total War in 1914 and the railways were now learning about it the hard way.

The London, Brighton & South Coast operated out of Newhaven and one of its finest steamers of the Edwardian era was the turbine-powered Dieppe. *She acted as a troop carrier in the first conflict but did not survive the second, by which time she had been sold out of railway service. She was mined off Tobruk in March 1941.*

The member railways which made up the Railway Executive Committee at the time of World War One comprised twelve, although the LBSCR and GER were not immediately admitted. The membership was largely as would be expected, including eleven of the fourteen companies shown in Table II as contributing vessels for naval usage, minus the Furness, G&SWR and North British. (The Great Northern made up the twelve, while the North Eastern's part-owned vessels do not appear to have interested the Admiralty initially, possibly because they were heavily engaged in the coal trade). As it happened, the LYR's General Manager was unable to take his seat on the Committee when it began as he had been unwise enough to take his holidays in Germany! He was not released until the end of September 1914.

The inclusion of the Caledonian Railway as Scottish representative in the REC at the expense of the North British was doubly curious. Not only was the NBR the larger company in terms of mileage and number of locomotives, it was appointed as 'Secretary Company' to the War Office's Scottish Command, an appointment which might reasonably have been anticipated for a company headquartered at Edinburgh, the Command centre, while the NB also served Rosyth, home to Admiral Beatty's scouting forces and, later in the war, to the entire Grand Fleet. As a result of this anomaly, neither of the Secretary Companies to the Scottish or Irish Army Commands were members of the railways' policy-making body. (See Table II).

A series of some 2,000 numbered circulars was sent out to the railway companies by the new Executive Committee over the years to the end of 1919 and an analysis of the first 100 confirms evidence that in 1914 the Admiralty had taken Lady Macbeth's advice to "stand not upon the order of your going, but go at once", and had begun ship requisitions immediately without recourse to the new REC. This was understandable, as the Committee was still establishing control, or rather the Government's control, over the nation's railways. Indeed, fewer than two per cent of the earliest REC circulars (some of which were sub-divided) dealt with shipping at all. No.7 advised the companies just two days into the war that the Board of Trade was no longer insisting on a survey of every ship before renewing marine certificates. Curiously, this announcement was based on the experience of one company, the South Eastern & Chatham, so the REC was effectively acting as a newsletter distributor for its controlled companies, when an announcement from the Board of Trade might have been more appropriate, particularly when the REC was a department of the Board.

The second relevant circular, No.86A, was more direct; effectively a census form for each company owning ships to register them, and their details, with the Executive Committee. Information requested (to be supplied in duplicate) comprised a list of ships owned, those already 'taken up', those required by the owning company to maintain ordinary services and any special tasks, and finally, 'those which are to spare'. Tonnage was to be specified for each vessel and should indicate whether it was configured for passengers or cargo. Potential speed capability was not asked about, but one suspects would have been of crucial importance to a more military-minded enquirer, since this would instantly decide if a vessel could undertake fleet work or would operate in a support capacity.

Issued at the end of September, this survey came too late to assist in the initial call-up of railway vessels at the outbreak of war, and had no effect on the Admiralty's requisitioning activities. The records show that two Great Western inshore vessels were requisitioned even before July 1914 was out, while the four major LNWR ferries plying the Irish Sea were in the hands of the Royal Navy within five days of war being declared on 4th August. By October four-fifths of the Great Western's Weymouth fleet had been requisitioned, so clearly the REC 'census' of available railway ships at the end of September was little more than a 'sweeping up' operation. Table III summarises the initial take-up of railway vessels by the middle of the first month of war.

A rare view of the seaplane carrier HMS Empress *being bombed by Germans on the Christmas Day raid on Cuxhaven. The photograph was taken from* Undaunted *which put two Zeppelins out of action with her anti-aircraft guns.*

"Lady Rowena" in war service

Lady Rowena *was a typical paddle steamer adapted for service in World War One. Ordered by the North British Railway in 1891 for the Loch Long route, she was sold to Italian owners in 1903, finding her way back to non-railway owners on the Clyde. She then undertook war service, mainly as a fleet tender on the Forth, and does not appear to have resumed civilian service in Scottish waters.*

With all main line railways immediately taken over by the Railway Executive Committee in 1914, their ship fleets were now effectively Government-controlled, so assurances against financial and shipwreck loss were all that required to be concluded. On the first of these points, the railways were offered guaranteed ship earnings equal to their net revenue of 1913, while, on the second, the Government would be responsible for all ship losses due to 'war risks'. This was to prove a definition open to question, since all voyages, even in peacetime, were potentially dangerous in the days before radio and radar, satellite navigation and weather-forecasting. The railways would be responsible for the 'ordinary' risks posed by the sea, unless a ship had been diverted from its usual routes for military reasons – which was frequently to be the case.

Compensation for loss at sea was a subject not easily settled and REC circulars were still featuring the subject long after war had been declared. In November 1916,

the railways were told in Circular 729 that "direct cash payments will not be made by the Admiralty, War Office, or Ministry of Munitions, the cost being charged in normal course to working expenses and recovered through the operation of guarantee". In other words, the REC would undertake to pass on compensation, although this would still leave the military to deal with non-railway shipowners: hardly a satisfactory procedure for any of those concerned. Not surprisingly, a Ministry of Shipping was established before the year was out (and re-established in 1939 within two months of the second conflict being declared). Incidentally, no-one could accuse the Executive Committee of sentimentality in its consideration of marine loss. The citing of compensation arrangements for the loss of railway ships was listed by the Committee in a table below the loss of income from rental premises, or through the compulsory carriage of timber.

Not all shipping lines insured with Lloyd's, indeed Great Central historian George Dow believed that this company was one of the 'very few' railways to do so. One which used smaller insurance concerns was the Caledonian Steam Packet Company – the marine 'arm' of the Caledonian Railway. In December 1914 the 'Caley' was insuring its 24-year old paddle steamer *Marchioness of Lorne* for £10,000 but its flagship, the turbine-driven *Duchess of Argyll,* was covered for three times that amount in the following February, in each case with a commercial insurer, Ewart & Co. In the following June (1915), the Admiralty confirmed compensation

The Duchess of Rothesay *served in both world wars, the first principally in the English Channel, where she captured a downed Zeppelin and rescued crews from no fewer than fifteen sinking ships. She is seen here in wartime 'uniform', with a sailor semaphoring from above her bridge.*

---

arrangements to the satisfaction of the CSP board – on which the railway Chairman was a director – so the company immediately cancelled its own policies for the *'Duchesses'* of Argyll, Hamilton and Montrose. Sadly, the last two named would be lost in this war, both of them in seas where they would normally never have operated. Four other 'Caley' steamers were insured commercially for a total of £55,000 by early 1916, but 'war risks' were not covered in the policy; as it happened, none of these other company steamers failed to return. Interestingly, when the Great Central lost its steamer *Immingham* in support of the Dardanelles campaign, it requested £100,000 compensation (obviously for a larger ship than the 'Caley' steamers). It had to settle for £45,000.

As the war went on, allowance was also made for companies having to seek replacement vessels to maintain the more important ferry or trading routes when they had lost most of their fleet to the military. The alternative to this might have been for the Admiralty to take only a particular number, or proportion, of ships from each company, and here the Railway Executive

Committee could have been expected to play a more active role. It hardly seemed worthwhile having a dedicated committee structure, such as the REC, liaising between railways and the military if it could not solve such elementary problems as over-reliance on one particular company's fleet while another's had capacity available.

But any 'evening-up' was left to the companies themselves; an obvious example was the Great Eastern's chartering of Great Central vessels from early in the conflict, the former company facing increased traffic challenges to the Netherlands and Belgium, while the latter had lost its German destinations. The Great Central itself was forced to charter at one stage of the war. Unable to repair a dredger because all Humber yards were already working to capacity, the GCR hired a Tilbury-based vessel (from a non-railway source). Unfortunately, it was mined on its voyage northwards to the Humber, and the North Eastern's dredger *Lord Joicey* was hurriedly chartered to replace it. As previously mentioned, the Great Western had four ferries taken off a single route, Weymouth–Channel Islands, in the first October of the war – and one was lost within four months.

It certainly appears that in most cases the Admiralty dealt directly with the companies themselves, without any reference to the Railway Executive Committee even when it was fully established and, as Pratt pointed out, "without any regard for the ability of the said companies to provide for essential services they were under obligation to maintain". The Admiralty even advised

that some vessels might not be returned at all, those which the naval authorities decided to retain being treated as losses for compensation purposes. Restoration was also a Government responsibility, with the companies to be given a twice-yearly report on the state of their ships while in military use, although there was a warning that it might not be worthwhile to repair or restore certain vessels after the Royal Navy had finished with them, never mind the enemy! Nevertheless, the six-monthly frequency timetable for reports gives an interesting contrast to the then-popular conception that the war would be over by Christmas 1914.

The lack of an overall transport ministry must have become an increasingly obvious problem as the war went on, and its establishment does appear to have been something of a priority for Lloyd George's government elected in December 1918. The Ministry became a legal reality on 15th August 1919, its title during the Parliamentary stages being the 'Ministry of Ways and Communications'. Sir Eric Geddes, previously Assistant General Manager of the North Eastern Railway, was the first Minister.

Although one of the smallest pre-grouping companies, the G&SWR maintained a fine fleet of steamers and they were nearly all requisitioned. One of the most attractive was the Glen Rosa, *normally sailing out of Ardrossan or Fairlie. During World War One she swept mines in Belfast Lough, her name being temporarily changed to* Glencross.

All the rail companies operating ships, either directly or through an "arm's length" company, lost vessels in World War One. But there is no suggestion that the railways bore a disproportionate or unfair burden in the supply of ships taken up. The non-railway Isle of Man Steam Packet Company, for example, gave up eleven of its fifteen steamers and one was lost in historic circumstances, as related in the text. What *was* unfair was the fact that railway seamen were paid less than their fellow-seamen and this is dealt with in the chapter on the events of the year 1918.

The Great Central lost three ships to German internment and chartered others from time to time to the Great Eastern, but one which had a quiet war between 1914-18 was the Dewsbury. *But this was a long-lived vessel and she braved dangerous waters in the second conflict as a rescue ship in the Battle of the Atlantic before continuing to sail the North Sea in the subsequent peace, notching up nearly 50 years' service, latterly with Associated Humber Lines, a company 90% owned by the BTC.*

While her GCR sister ship Macclesfield *survived both wars and completed 44 years of service up to 1958,* Chesterfield *was less fortunate. Towards the end of the first war she was painted in a 'dazzle' camouflage scheme, intended to confuse U-boat commanders selecting a target ship via a periscope. It was later learned that this ploy had been ineffectual, but the crews of ships so painted felt safer!*

Another Clyde paddler which attained half a century of service, the Duchess of Fife *joined the Caledonian fleet in 1903. In World War One she served as a minesweeper on the east coast, while in the second, she joined the Harwich flotilla which was ordered to Dunkirk in May 1940. She survived this, and the rest of the war, before returning to civilian service with British Railways until 1953.*

This stern shot of HMS Engadine, *the SECR ferry pressed into war service within a week of the declaration in 1914, shows the hangar built to house seaplanes. These were lowered into, and lifted out of, the sea when reconnaissance was required. Although it could take up to half an hour to 'launch' a plane, the* Engadine *was able to supply information to Admiral Beatty at the outset of the Battle of Jutland. She went on to save nearly 700 men from the sinking* HMS Warrior *during the battle.*

HMS Engadine, *in fact an SECR railway ferry, is seen undertaking her wartime role as a seaplane carrier, one she contributed uniquely at the Battle of Jutland in 1916. Her hangar was a wartime fitting, removed before she resumed her ferrying duties in later years up to 1933, and her White Ensign is prominent above. The Royal Navy must have been well satisfied with* Engadine, *giving the same name to a 1960s-built helicopter carrier which served in the Falklands conflict.*

No distinction is made, in the chronological narrative which follows, between railway ships operating under the White Ensign of the Royal Navy and those which continued in a civilian role. (The fleet lists at the end of this book indicate where naval service was undergone. Direct purchase by the Admiralty, as opposed to temporary requisitioning, is indicated where known). There are two reasons for not differentiating between those railways taken up and those still fulfilling their civilian functions. Firstly, ships sailing in wartime were at the mercy of shared dangers. Mines were no respecters of civilian status; neither were enemy warships if their captains suspected that a merchant ship or ferry was carrying military supplies or personnel. In addition, lighthouses were often closed and weather ships withdrawn, thus doubling the potential dangers of the most routine voyage. Secondly, many civilian ships *did* carry military supplies and personnel to and from war zones. Soldiers' mail could come into this category and there is evidence (as in the case of the doomed *Anglia* in 1915) of emergency or unscheduled requisitioning of vessels.

The story of railway ships in World War One is told on a year-by-year basis, while that of the second conflict is told in a less formal chronology, focusing principally on major operations such as the evacuations from Europe, the Dieppe raid and D-Day, while also examining the new dangers ships faced from aircraft and influence mines, in addition to submarines and the pronged contact mine. Looking back, there is a clear progression to be seen in maritime aspects of World War Two – from defeat and retreat in Europe, to spasmodic attempts to re-invade, followed by a full-scale amphibious operation. Railway ships were involved in all of these. In contrast, the opening of 1918, the final year of World War One was indistinguishable from that of, say, 1915, 1916 or 1917. There was a stalemate in the affairs of war, so a more detailed survey of each year repays study.

Chapter 4
WORLD WAR ONE – YEAR BY YEAR

1914

On 6th August 1914, only 48 hours after Britain and Germany had entered what soon became known as the Great War, a steamer owned by the Great Eastern Railway cast off from Harwich for the Netherlands. One of her passengers was the German ambassador to the UK, and once arrived at the Hook of Holland the *St. Petersburg* awaited the arrival of his German-based counterpart, the British ambassador from Berlin, before heading back across the North Sea.

It was the final act in the ending of diplomatic relations between the two nations for nearly five years, during which millions were to die. The *St. Petersburg* herself was to survive this conflict, but not the second war against Germany. Renamed *Archangel,* she was sunk by Luftwaffe aircraft with much loss of life, 27 years later in that century of two total wars.

The 4th August 1914 was the date of Britain's ultimatum to Germany expiring, but Britain's railway ships were to experience the onrush of war before even a shot was fired. On that date, three Great Central vessels set off from Hamburg, desperately trying to reach home waters before Britain's ultimatum to Germany expired at eleven o'clock that night. The three were the *City of Bradford, City of Leeds* and the *Bury*. Arrested by German patrol craft in the Elbe, the ships were forced to return to port, their crews, totalling 89, being interned at Ruhleben, a former racecourse-turned-internment camp near Berlin. Three of the crews were women stewardesses, whom the Germans released. (GCR ships were basically freighters with limited passenger accommodation, as the 375-mile Grimsby –Hamburg run was too long and insufficiently lucrative for passenger ferrying alone.)

In his definitive history of the GCR, George Dow states categorically that the ships were stopped *before* the expiry of the 4th August ultimatum in 1914, giving Edwin Pratt as his source, although the latter fails to confirm that point. This was entirely possible in any event; German forces had already invaded Belgium and Russian-held Poland by that date, irrespective of the time-limit specified by the British ultimatum. Of course, Germany was an hour ahead of the UK in terms of time-zones, then as now, so whether the arrests were 'legal' or not is unclear. Another railway steamer, the Lancashire & Yorkshire's *Dearne* was similarly seized, but unlike the GCR vessels, was put to use by its new 'owners'. These incidents were not reported in *The Times* newspaper, an otherwise meticulous recorder of ship casualties in the years to come.

What is undeniable is that the railway crews were condemned to more than four years of imprisonment, which a number of them failed to survive. At least the crewmen could partake of cricket, football and musical events (only Russians appear to have been maltreated at Ruhleben) and they were spared ordeal by mine and torpedo, which was to afflict so many of their fellow merchant seaman, and indeed, many of their fellow GCR and LYR employees. Not until November 1918 were these railway ships restored to their owners, although 'the enemy', as the Germans technically were until the summer of 1919, delivered the three GCR vessels to the 'wrong' estuary – the Tyne. The *Dearne* was at the bottom of the sea by then, as will be related.

Two days after the British declaration of war, the Great Eastern was responsible, as mentioned above, for transporting the German ambassador to the Court of St. James back to the Continent via Harwich and the Hook of Holland. He later recorded his appreciation of the courtesy shown to him and his household by the railway's employees on train and ship. This was in sharp contrast to the experience of the British ambassador in Berlin. He and his family had to struggle with their own luggage through an angry crowd after the embassy's German servants had refused to assist the 'enemy'. In view of the later tussles between GER ships and German U-boats, both ambassadors were lucky they did not find themselves forced into lifeboats in the open sea. Until the following February, a rigorous code of engagement, only after challenge, was pursued by both navies, but even that was to prove mortally dangerous to merchant and passenger ships especially if a U-Boat commander had reason to believe that a civilian ship was carrying combatants or logistical materials.

Nowadays it seems axiomatic that the UK should have a fast response military unit to protect the nation's interests overseas, or come to the aid of a territorial possession or an ally under attack, but this has only been the case for the last 60 years. In the nineteenth century, an overseas conflict – in the Crimea or South Africa, for example – would have involved a slow assembling of men, horses and material for eventual despatch to a far-off war in a fanfare of trumpets. Even in the early 1930s, British governments operated a 'Ten Year Rule', believing that any threat of war would allow sufficient time for rearming and this was to lead to the scrapping of many a warship. The existence of this policy after the (well-named) Great War is a matter for some surprise, to say the least.

For in 1906, with Europe criss-crossed by alliances, a Liberal government realised that a quicker response might be required to any international crisis, and one result of a major War Office reorganisation by Robert Haldane was the British Expeditionary Force. This was an almost self-contained army consisting of six infantry divisions and one of cavalry. On 6th August, only two days after Britain's declaration of war, it was decided to send this force, minus one infantry unit, to assist the French. This was not a unanimous decision, with both Prime Minister Asquith and Foreign Secretary Sir Edward Grey opposed to their going at all. But the die was cast, with a military timetable already agreed. Indeed, historian A. J. P. Taylor has argued that World War One was inevitable once military mobilisations took place in the nations concerned, as railway timetables were immediately printed and were then rigidly adhered to by a level of management not in contact with the ruling elites. By the 9th of the month, the transport of five of the six divisions had begun, no matter what the Prime Minister may have thought.

The logistical challenge of moving the British Expeditionary Force was formidable. Train and ship had to deliver to France around 120,000 officers and men, nearly 38,000 horses, 314 artillery pieces, 5,000 tons of stores and not forgetting 1,807 bicycles. Southampton was chosen as the main port of transit, a fact not unconnected with the appointment of the London & South Western Railway as the 'Secretary company' for railways in the south of England dealing with the War Office's Southern Command. Incidentally, the Railway Executive Committee had only begun work the previous week, its first 'Instruction' going out to member companies on 31st July. None of these irregular but frequent circulars from the REC dealt with this mobilisation, although later ones featured the transporting of parcels to the BEF.

The first train reached the embarkation quay on Sunday 10th at 8.15am, 33 minutes early. Over one subsequent fourteen-hour period a train arrived at the quayside every twelve minutes – 73 of them – each being cleared and moved out empty in seven minutes. Only 150 feet separated ship and train, allowing immediate loading. (Although Southampton was the principal port of embarkation, the SECR vessel *Hythe* was to claim having landed the first British troops in France.) The last of the first wave of BEF units reached Southampton at 6.00pm on 10th August, 22 minutes early. One of the five infantry divisions was kept in the UK by a Government grown increasingly uneasy watching the impressive German march into Belgium – and this infantry reallocation in itself necessitated a logistically-challenging transfer from Ireland to Great Britain – but the BEF had to be reinforced almost immediately.

This cross-Channel transfer represented, according to official naval historian Sir Julian Corbett, "a task which in difficulty and magnitude was quite beyond its [the Admiralty's] experience". It was, however, not quite unprecedented – the French had brought their Algerian army group across the Mediterranean only days before – but that was too recent for any lessons to be learned. The French had escorted their transport ships, something the British failed to do. Instead, each ship sailed once loaded at Southampton and proceeded alone to Le Havre. The Royal Navy provided distant cover, units of the Channel fleet sealing the approaches to east and west, with the French providing destroyers to supplement the Dover Patrol. The Channel Fleet comprised no fewer than nineteen battleships, with attendant cruisers and destroyers, or 'Torpedo Boat Destroyers', as they were called in those days.

This impressive weight of armour was, of course, quite independent of the Grand Fleet, kept at readiness at Scapa Flow in the Orkneys to challenge the German High Seas Fleet if it should move against the transports. In fact, Count von Moltke, Chief of the German General Staff, was later quoted as saying that he was quite happy to see the British army cross to France so that it could be destroyed there at the same time as the French, all as part of the Schlieffen Plan to win the war in the west before turning on the slower-to-mobilise Russia.

Looking back, it seems obvious that both sides underestimated the damage the submarine could do against unprotected ships, whether naval or civilian. Within six weeks, a single U-Boat, captained by a commander with no combat experience, sank three British cruisers in the Channel in a single night, with enormous loss of life. As the steamers of the LSWR were carrying troops, they would have been legitimate

S.S. "ATALANTA".

Unlike all the other G&SWR ships, the Atalanta *was a turbine vessel, undertaking war service in World War One as both a trooper and a minesweeper at different times, latterly at Harwich. Sold out of LMS service in 1937, she was used for boom defence work in the second conflict.*

targets for a submarine, committed at that time to rules of engagement which involved challenge before attack, but only if the target was identified as civilian.

Yet Corbett, while listing the battleships of the Channel Fleet – more than the whole Royal Navy had available in World War Two – does not mention a single railway, or other civilian, steamer by name when participating in the transfer of the BEF to France. And by voyaging unescorted through narrow waters where submarines could, and later did, operate, they were taking a terrible risk. The reintroduction of LSWR sailings to and from Le Havre on 19th September suggests either ignorance of modern warfare, which would be understandable, or sheer bravado, which was not. Fate was in fact kind to the South Western, with none of its ships lost to submarine before January 1918. Ironically, despite the logistical triumph of the cross-Channel transfer, so much dependent on the efficiency of

such civilian ship crews as those of the London & South Western Railway, the enemy was hardly overawed by the size of the British contingent. The Kaiser commented on this 'contemptibly small army' – giving rise to the later nickname, borne with pride – of the 'Old Contemptibles' – while the Germans revived the old Bismarck joke of sending the police to arrest the British!

The authorities at home, civilian and military, were nevertheless impressed by the BEF move. Minister for War Kitchener was quoted as saying on 25th August, when reinforcements were still arriving, that "the railway companies, in the all-important matter of transport facilities, have more than justified the complete confidence reposed in them by the War Office". The BEF commander, the appropriately-named Sir John French, confirmed in mid-September that "the transport of troops from England, both by sea and by rail, was affected in the best order and without a check. Each unit arrived at its destination in this country well within the scheduled time".

This punctuality was no trivial matter. On 23rd August the BEF found itself under crushing attack at Mons from a numerically superior German force. Although forced to retreat, the British were able to slow the enemy advance, and, with their French allies, halt it altogether on the River Marne, thus introducing a period of stalemate that was to last for years. If the BEF had not been in place so quickly, the War might have taken a different turn.

The Belgian port of Antwerp gained in importance in 1914 once Brussels was overrun, and the Baltic closed to allied shipping, but it was not long out of the firing-line itself. Bombed by airships before August was over, the city became a strategic target for ground forces when Germany abandoned its Schlieffen Plan and had to settle for a long campaign in northern France and the Low Countries. Driving to the sea made sense to the invaders, since Antwerp could be used as a base to attack British supply lines linked to the Channel ports to the south. Early in October, the German attack began on this, the temporary capital of Belgium.

British troops rushed to the city, many of them arriving at Ostend with London buses as transport, some of them still showing such destinations on their screens as 'Bank' and 'Piccadilly'. Winston Churchill, a former (and future) soldier, although now First Lord of the Admiralty, travelled to Antwerp to see things for himself – and was not impressed. The French failed to send a promised force, so the British also decided not to commit as many troops as they had intended to reinforce the Royal Naval Division. Meanwhile, German and Austrian artillery caused terrible damage and suffering, almost without reply, and the city fathers prepared to surrender.

On 7th October, with howitzer shells falling around, two Great Eastern ships made final preparations to leave Antwerp. One of these was the *Brussels,* whose name will certainly recur in the story of North Sea operations in World War One, but last of all was the company's steamer *Amsterdam.* This Hull-built vessel cast off into the Scheldt with Belgian refugees on board as well as the British Consul-General. And none too soon. Within hours, 60,000 German troops marched through Antwerp in triumph. No allied vessel visited again until 17th December 1918, when the same diplomat returned on board another GER vessel (actually the *Marylebone,* chartered from the Great Central).

Lloyd's published records of ships sunk, captured or damaged in World War One annotates the loss of the cargo ship *Glitra* in October as the first 'vessel' sunk by a submarine (although presumably civilian vessel is meant. U9's trio of cruiser victims were despatched in the Channel in September 1914, a month earlier, with HMS *Pathfinder,* the earliest victim of all, sunk in the Forth by U21 on 5th September). The Leith-registered *Glitra* was torpedoed after challenge when carrying coal from Grangemouth to Stavanger on 20th October, but her crew had been given time to scramble into lifeboats and were then towed towards the Norwegian coast by her conquerers. (This humanitarian gesture was also made in the following year to the crew of the LNWR's *Hibernia,* although with less happy results). Six days later there was a greater potential disaster when the French steamer *Amiral Ganteaume* was torpedoed without warning while carrying refugees from the Lille and Arras areas to safety. A tragedy was averted thanks to the South Eastern & Chatham ferry *The Queen,* which went alongside the French ship and took off 2,200 passengers within 30 minutes. This was not the last act of gallantry from the master and crew of this railway ship, and she deserved a better fate than befell her in the autumn of 1916, as will be related.

Meanwhile, the months of August and September 1914 had seen the loss of four trawlers when minesweeping. At that time, two vessels were required to operate together, dragging a trawl-wire behind them in an attempt to cut the moorings (or 'sinkers') of concealed mines. Naval historian A. D. Divine wrote in 1940 that, for every two mines destroyed in 1914, a minesweeper was lost. By 1918, 80 mines could be swept for every loss. It was certainly a hard way to acquire expertise and although railway vessels did not suffer losses in the early days of minesweeping, it would prove just as deadly for them over the next four years.

A fortnight before Christmas, the Great Eastern's ship *Colchester,* although operating under company colours, encountered a U-Boat off the Hook of Holland. Piling on all speed, the two-funnelled veteran steamer fled the surfaced submarine for all of twenty minutes before the hunter gave up the chase. It was a frightening experience for her crew and passengers. Unfortunately, much worse was to befall Britain's merchant steamers in the following year.

The year 1915 at sea introduced two major developments, both of which involved merchant ships requisitioned by the Royal Navy, as well as those continuing commercial trading. The first was the declaration by the Germans in February of unrestricted submarine warfare in the seas around the British Isles, the second was the Dardanelles campaign. Both these events began in the third week of February, within a twenty-four hour period, but their effect was to last for most of the war.

On 15th February, the Germans announced that they were introducing unrestricted submarine warfare in British waters. Until that time, a German U-boat sighting what appeared to be a civilian vessel would surface and challenge it to identify itself. If it turned out to be British, or belonging to a country allied to Britain, the crew would be ordered into their lifeboats and the ship sunk. This would be done by gunfire if possible, in order to save torpedoes, particularly if the hull was wooden and could be easily penetrated by gunfire or bombs (as hand grenades were called at the time). Many civilian ships were still not fitted with radio, but if so, the crew would be warned not to call for help. But as from 18th February, the Germans reserved the right to attack without warning (although there was to be an interregnum between September 1915 and January 1917).

The most illustrious target to suffer in this new campaign was the trans-Atlantic Cunarder *Lusitania,* torpedoed in early May with a loss of nearly 1,200 civilian lives, one-tenth of them American. It did not take much imagination to see that this policy was not going to encourage the United States to abandon its neutrality in German's favour and a more liberal policy by the German Admiralty would have been in her own interests. The first German attack on an American ship had in fact happened only a week previously on 1st May, the United States tanker *Gulflight* having been torpedoed by U-6 while on route from Port Arthur to Rouen. Although she had been towed to safety in the Isles of Scilly, according to Lloyd's records, *The Times* announced her as a total loss, with the Germans admitting culpability and offering to pay an indemnity. This would not restore her dead captain, however.

German submarine commanders frequently used their initiative in their method of attack, often continuing to challenge after surfacing – indeed the German determination to save torpedoes wherever possible gave the Royal Navy the tactical opportunity of employing Q-Boats from November 1914. These were pseudo-merchantmen bearing hidden guns, which opened up when the submarine had surfaced. One of the first of these was the Great Eastern's *Vienna,* temporarily renamed *Antwerp* and later *Roulers,* deployed to linger in North Sea areas where ships had already been attacked. She signally failed to attract a single predator, being replaced by vessels such as the *Baralong,* which historians seemed to believe was more suitable for the task. In fact, judging by the frequency with which GER vessels were targeted on their regular shuttles, it would appear that the Admiralty's initial choice of ship was perfectly reasonable. By the end of hostilities, eleven U-Boats had been destroyed by 'Mystery Ships' as one of their captains called them; indeed the account of these operations, written by Captain Campbell, one of their commanders, is grotesquely light-hearted in its tone. Any success must be measured against the possible effect their use had; Q-boats simply gave the Germans an added incentive to attack without warning from nderwater. It is possible that many crewmen and passengers perished because of the Q-Boat policy.

The first railway steamer to be sunk in World War One was well north of its usual haunts. The Admiralty had decided that the trawlers entrusted with the task of sowing mines outside and around Scapa Flow, base to the Grand Fleet, were too slow to cover the area required, so the Great Western Railway had four of its Channel Islands steamers requisitioned and given the necessary modifications for minelaying at very short notice. This precautionary initiative appeared all the more necessary when a U-boat had to be driven off by destroyer from one of the Orkney approaches on 3rd December 1914. The GWR four (*Reindeer, Roebuck, Lynx* and *Gazelle*) were hurriedly put to work, along with the other 'steam packets' as they were called in the official naval history – *Folkestone* and *Hythe* of the SECR, and the *Clacton* and *Newmarket* from the GER.

Unfortunately the *Roebuck*, now renamed *Roedean*, sank in Scapa Flow less than a fortnight into the new year. (There already was an HMS *Roebuck*, a 1901 Tyne-built destroyer which would survive the war, while *Lynx* was renamed *Lynn* as another destroyer carried that name before being sunk by mine in August 1915). The loss of the GWR vessel was attributed to various causes. In their book *Railway and Other Steamers,* Messrs, Duckworth and Langmuir blame torpedoing by a German submarine which, given the location, would have caused a panic at the Admiralty, if true. Edwin Pratt suggests a collision with a French battleship attached to the Grand Fleet, but Lloyd's listing carries a more likely explanation – a mine, and (although not

A railway paddle steamer which never sailed in anything but naval grey was the Fair Maid, *ordered by the North British but requisitioned straight out of the shipyard in 1915. She became one of the last rail sinkings in 1916, mined in the North Sea in November of that year. Her near-sister,* Waverley, *survived this war, only to succumb to air attack in the next.*

stated) probably a 'friendly' device, drifting from where it had been sown for anchorage protection, quite possibly by one of the four GWR steamers themselves. The *Reindeer* was to survive a major collision in the war, later being purchased by the Admiralty, and then sold off in 1920. *Gazelle* and *Lynn* reappear in the Official History of naval operations in 1918, sailing the classic waters of the Aegean.

Meanwhile, sister ship *Ibex* (although technically the only one of her class) continued on her company station operating out of Weymouth. This tough little two-funnel ship had already survived a sinking off Guernsey, remaining 'on the bottom' for some six months in 1900, but was credited by Edwin Pratt with having later sunk a U-boat by gunfire while in (supposedly) civilian use. It took more than a sinking to finish off at least one Great Western ship!

Away from British waters, civilian shipping was about to supplement naval forces in another theatre of war. British commanders, encouraged by First Lord of the Admiralty Winston Churchill, decided to open a new front by attacking Germany's ally Turkey, on 19th February 1915. This would be done by landing troops on the Gallipoli peninsula, just south-west of where the Dardanelles straits separate Europe and Asia. It was a good idea in theory, but muddled organisation, coupled with a disdain for the fighting qualities of the enemy – always a fatal attitude to take into a conflict – led to a stalemate which almost mirrored that of the Western Front.

"Hospital ships were soon to be as familiar a sight in the Eastern Mediterranean as warships", writes historian Sir Martin Gilbert of the situation in late April, when, for every three men successfully landed in fighting order on the peninsula, two were already evacuating out wounded.

The landings which began in February had variable success, some beaches being undefended by the Turks while others were nothing less than killing grounds for the unfortunate British and Imperial (as then described) infantry. Command of this amphibious operation was conducted by General Sir Ian Hamilton from, to begin with, a capital ship in the outer cordon and then from a Greek island. Needless to say, the operation was doomed to failure, particularly with the Turks producing a commander, Mustafa Kemal, as efficient as Hamilton was inept. Coincidentally, one of the principal bombarding battleships was HMS *Lord Nelson,* flagship of the Channel Fleet in the previous August. In writing about SECR ships operating off Gallipoli, Edwin Pratt records matter-of-factly that the railway steamers proved useful for "drawing enemy fire away from the battleships"! The Official History, in describing naval operations in this area, continued its usual policy of not troubling to name civilian ships in support.

Railway ships came into their own in this theatre after the first outbreak of fighting had died down, contributing as supply ships and taking off the wounded. Despite this non-military role, three of them were never to leave Mediterranean waters. The Great Central's *Immingham* was a handsome 2,000-tonner built to operate to and from the Continent out of Grimsby, but soon found herself in more exotic surroundings. But not for long. Adapted twice in six months for Admiralty service, the second time as recently as the previous April, this Tyne-built ship was in use as a stores carrier when

sunk in a fatal collision off the island of Mudros on 6th June. This was the first of two accidents exclusively involving railway vessels, the other ship in this collision being the HMS *Reindeer,* normally a Great Western ferry on the Channel Islands run. The Great Central requested £100,000 compensation for its loss, but had to settle for £45,000. A tragic irony is evident in one of the last pre-war advertisements for Grimsby–Rotterdam services operated by the *Immingham.* The travelling public had been advised that she was fitted with Stone Lloyd's Patent Watertight Doors which could be closed from the bridge in only eight seconds, "thus ensuring the absolute safety of the steamer".

Also present at the Dardanelles campaign was the South Eastern & Chatham Railway's Clyde-built freighter *Hythe,* and she was involved in evacuating Australian troops from the holocaust of Suvla Bay. On 28th October, she collided in darkness with the *Sarnia* and foundered in waters off Greece. The latter vessel, requisitioned from the LSWR, was not to survive Mediterranean service either, torpedoed only two months before the 1918 Armistice.

Another victim of the new war theatre was the *Hibernia,* the first vessel of the London & North Western Railway to be lost. Armed and renamed HMS *Tara,* she was far from her Holyhead–Dublin run when torpedoed by U35 in Sollum Bay, Egypt, on Guy Fawkes' Day, 1915. 34 crew members were reported lost, but one lifeboat was said to have reached the North African shore, and *The Times* announced on the 22nd of the month that survivors had been reported in the area of El Aziat, and were 'all well'. The newspaper was clearly having to rely on foreign sources of information, but published a Foreign Office assurance that Egyptian-based diplomats were doing their utmost to locate the survivors. They then faded from the newspaper columns, just another group of men, it seemed, caught up in the whirlwind of war.

Nowadays we have the benefit of reading the diary of HMS *Tara* crewman David John Davies, preserved in the Anglesey public archives. He recorded that they "were making for Sollum, an Egyptian port on the border of Egypt and Libya. The Ship was Torpedoed on the Starboard side of the engine at about 10.10 a.m. in the morning and sank about seven minutes later... the Torpedo was reported by the look-out man in the crow's nest who saw it coming towards [us]. The helm was put over but as the ship was only travelling at about 7½ knots per hour, she refused to answer her helm... The submarine was seen some distance away and nine rounds was [were] fired at her, but all missed the target".

It appeared that no fewer than 93 of the 104 crewmen survived the explosion, and the U35 towed the lifeboats towards Port Suliman – a generous action considering that the *Tara* had opened fire on her. Unfortunately, the crew – mainly from Anglesey – appear then to have been taken prisoners by nomads who forced the men to accompany them on a march through harrowing desert conditions. They were not rescued until the following 17th March when a British column of armoured cars discovered them by chance. They were taken to hospital in Alexandria and eventually returned to a hero's welcome in Anglesey, apart from one unfortunate crewmen who had died following amputation of a leg.

But home waters were no safer. Narrowly avoiding a watery berth at the bottom of the sea that spring was the North Eastern's *Kirkham Abbey,* piling on all steam, like the GER's *Colchester,* to successfully escape a surfaced U-Boat in the North Sea. But there was no favourable outcome for the LSWR's *Guernsey*, wrecked on the French coast in April because a lighthouse was darkened. While not on military service, there was no doubt that this 41 year-old railway freighter was another victim of war. The next two losses occurred within 48 hours of each other in the North Sea. On 6th May, the North Eastern's *Truro,* now under non-railway ownership, was torpedoed by a U-Boat 85 miles off St. Abb's Head in Berwickshire. At least the crew survived, being taken prisoner by a submarine commander who was notably humane in sparing their lives, particularly since his weapon of choice to confer the *coup de grace* could have been fired underwater without warning anyway. Only two days later the *Don,* belonging to the Lancashire & Yorkshire, was torpedoed seven miles off Coquet Island, Northumberland, on route in ballast from Cromarty to Blyth. Her loss is located in Lloyd's published list only one place down from the *Lusitania.*

The LYR company would lose most of the vessels on its books before peace returned to the seas, and one of its ships which had been sold to the Isle of Man Steam Packet company, the *Duke of Lancaster,* was also sunk in the North Sea before summer was out. Renamed *Ramsey,* she succumbed to torpedo and gunfire from the German auxiliary cruiser *Meteor* off the Cromarty Firth on 8th August. It was a case of one requisitioned ship challenging another; the *Ramsey* was now officially an 'armed boarding cruiser' and had asked the *Meteor,* flying a Russian flag, to stop and allow inspection. The British crew were lowering a boat to approach her, when the German ship literally revealed her true colours.

The *Meteor* was a converted civilian steamer herself, previously the Currie Line vessel *Vienna* captured in Hamburg at the outset of war (and not to be confused with the Great Eastern ship of the same name). Now armed, she triggered a major military crisis in the North Sea in May 1915. Naval commanders were convinced that she was a serious threat as a minelayer, possibly because (and this was not mentioned in the official naval account of this incident) her civilian profile allowed her to penetrate British waters more easily, so they decided that the *Meteor* must be destroyed. At one time, no fewer than three patrolling flotillas, totalling twelve cruisers, were sweeping the North Sea to locate her – three times as many as hunted the pocket battleship *Graf Spee* in the next war! When the *Meteor* was located making for Germany with the Ramsey's crew aboard, two Zeppelins were seen deployed by the Germans to warn her that the pursuers were closing. Within 24 hours of sinking the Isle of Man ship, the Germans decided to scuttle their own and British cruisers arrived in time to see the Leith-built enemy vanish beneath the waves.

Although it has no immediate bearing on the history of the railway steamers, what happened next provided an amusing coda to the incident, and illustrated some of the problems facing civilian crews caught up in war. German and British crews in the *Meteor's* lifeboats were rescued by a Swedish vessel, but since Sweden was neutral, an argument developed about who should be regarded as prisoners. Agreement was reached when the British were offered the chance to transfer to a Norwegian ship, but at the last minute they expressed concern about having no money. The Germans appear to have had a 'whip-round' for them! The Official History records that the money was repaid through diplomatic channels.

A sister ship to the *Hibernia* was the Dublin-registered *Anglia,* another LNWR vessel on the Holyhead–Dublin route. Taken up initially by the Navy, she is listed as having been released from the service by May 1915, but was certainly operating as a ferry and hospital ship in the Straits of Dover later that year, returning King George V home from France as recently as 28th October

The South Eastern & Chatham Railway was thanked by Field Marshall Haig in 1918 for its handling of logistical supplies to the British Army on the Continent. But as a soldier he appeared unaware of the company's contribution to the fighting strength of the Royal Navy, with three fast Channel steamers being requisitioned early in the war and none represented this contribution more than the Engadine, *delivered in 1911 and seen here in wartime garb.*

following the incident when he was injured by a fall from a horse when inspecting troops. He could have been in worse trouble than this; on 16th November, when bringing wounded back from France, the *Anglia* was mined only one mile from the safety of Folkestone. The death toll was heavy – accounts ranging from 134 to 251, including 'cot cases'. Worse was to follow immediately; a passing merchant vessel outward bound from London for Cadiz gallantly came to the rescue, only to run into the same minefield, capsizing quickly with an unknown death-toll. She was the 1,834-ton *Lusitania,* the second such to be sunk in that year. King George was shocked by the incident, writing a personal letter of sympathy to the First Lord of the Admiralty. (This suggests that the published release date of the *Anglia* from naval service is wrong, or that she had been hurriedly commandeered for this particular operation.) *Anglia* and *Hibernia* of the London & North Western Railway had been sunk within eleven days of each other, hundreds of miles apart. Their sisters *Cambria* and *Scotia* survived, the remaining pair of the four requisitioned so hurriedly in this war.

Meanwhile, reinforcing the Old was the New. A volunteer army had trained in Britain over the winter months, and in May was ready to be ferried to France. Three divisions totalling 100,000 men were transported over from Folkestone and Southampton, while others were being readied for the longer sea voyage to Gallipoli. It was starting to be a depressing time for the crews of the railway steamers whether requisitioned or continuing on Channel packet duties – bringing back the dead and wounded, then ferrying a shipload of young soldiers of the New Army to take their place in the battlefield.

The year came to a close with two more railway ship sinkings. The paddle steamer *Duchess of Hamilton,* which the Caledonian Steam Packet Company had just entrusted to the Government's insurance cover, was sunk by a mine off Harwich on 29th November, the day before St. Andrew's Day. The *Duchess* would never have operated in the North Sea in peacetime and her role as a minesweeper was a million miles away from its usual work as a pleasure steamer on the Firth of Clyde. The loss was formally noted by the Caledonian board on 14th December, when the directors decided to seek a tender from Denny's for a "similar steamer" and a weekly pension of £1 granted "if necessary" to a Mrs. Stark, widow of the ship's Second Engineer.

Less than a month later a particularly poignant sinking took place. This was the captured Great Central steamer *Dearne,* which had been seized by the Germans at Hamburg in August 1914. She was lost in the North Sea on 22nd December 1915 when being sailed by a German crew. Lloyd's list is not explicit about how she met her end and one possibility is scuttling after challenge, or with allied forces in the area. Her crew may have regarded the *Dearne* as expendable since she had not been a German ship in the first place.

istorians of World War One at sea regard the Battle of Jutland as the major naval conflict of the war. The clash of the British Grand and German High Seas Fleets had been anticipated from August 1914 and was regarded as the ultimate test of the nation, a chance to win the war with a single stroke or, as Churchill pointed out, to lose it in an afternoon.

In the event, the Battle of Jutland, which took place on 31st May/1st June 1916, was something of an anticlimax, with a damaged British fleet left bloody but unbowed on the battlefield while the enemy, with fewer losses in ships or men, returned to base, although not unscathed. Nearly 9,000 men on both sides were killed in less than a day, and some mighty warships were never seen again.

But not only capital ships were involved. While their story has been told and retold many times, less attention has been given to the role played by requisitioned vessels in support of the Grand Fleet, and at least one railway-owned steamer had a tale to tell. This was the *Engadine*, a triple-screw ferry owned by the South Eastern & Chatham and capable of a speed of 23 knots. Along with her sister *Riviera* and an older turbine *Empress III*, the *Engadine* became a fighting ship in World War One, allocated to operate alongside heavy naval units. She was particularly notable for serving with Admiral Beatty's battlecruiser squadron, patrolling out of the Firth of Forth with the support of five new 'Queen Elizabeth' battleships. This was not likely to be seen as a sinecure, given Beatty's known predilection to attack the enemy on sight, even if outnumbered and outgunned. In theory, Beatty's battlecruisers – armed like battleships, but with lighter armour and higher speed – were intended to attack and then withdraw to tempt the enemy on to the waiting Grand Fleet, but Beatty always attacked whether reinforced or not. And the South Eastern's *Engadine* was stationed plumb in the middle of this spoiling fighter's force on the day battle commenced.

Many railway ships were fitted for minesweeping, but it was a different kind of sweeping carried out by the three SECR turbines. Adapted as seaplane carriers, the ferries were fitted with cranes to lower their three aircraft into the sea if wave height was not excessive, and

the plane would taxi back to the ship when its patrol was over. Deck take-off and landing was not available on the *Engadine* and even catapult-launchings had not been introduced. The safety of the improvised carrier was obviously compromised by its having to slow and, when necessary for aircraft recovery, stop altogether. No less than 28 minutes was required to launch a plane to provide Beatty with information of the enemy's whereabouts and strength on 31st May, but within another twenty the first of three 'valuable and specific signals' was communicated. Her plane, piloted by Flight Lieutenant Frederick Rutland, was forced down because of a broken fuel pipe, but Rutland and his observer repaired this themselves, only to be refused permission to go up again.

Because of this limited manouverability, and because of their important role in providing invaluable aerial reconnaissance, *Engadine* and her sisters could have become priority targets for enemy scouting groups made up of destroyers and cruisers. Despite this, *Engadine* was to survive the war. Her counterpart with the Grand Fleet itself was the former Cunarder *Campania*, with a complement of ten planes and a flight deck for take-offs. Unfortunately, she was unable to participate in the coming battle at Jutland, failing to raise steam in time to leave Scapa with the battle fleet, and then ordered home with mechanical problems after three hours in trying to catch up with the leviathans. (This was the official version; historian Richard Hough believes that the ship did not receive the signal to sail from its remote anchorage within the Flow and her speed potential, which would have allowed her to catch up, was misreported to Admiral Jellicoe.)

As it was, *Engadine* of the South Eastern & Chatham Railway was about to make the only aerial contribution to the greatest naval battle of World War One. She managed to detect and then evade the enemy at Jutland, but the information gleaned by her aircraft made, or would have made if communications had been better, an important contribution to Beatty's role in the battle. This was considerable, his armoured ships engaging a superior force before the rest of the British fleet could give assistance. Three of his battlecruisers sank with

Train ferries were found to be necessary in World War One for ferrying rail vehicles over the Channel, using a new port at Richborough in Kent. These were Government-owned at first, being later purchased by the LNER for use at Harwich. This is a shot of one of the three vessels, described by historians Duckworth and Langmuir as "hideous" although these critical gentlemen conceded that they were "most useful", and proved so, in two wars.

terrible loss of life, prompting the Admiral's immortal comment "Something wrong with our bloody ships today." Beatty's own flagship was damaged – there was no question of this redoubtable commander remaining well away from the fighting, unlike so many army generals – and his new 'Queen Elizabeth' battleships in support (four of them; the name ship herself was in dockyard hands) all had to make a clumsy turning manoeuvre which allowed the entire enemy line to concentrate gunfire on each vessel one after another.

Firing between the two main fleets came later in the engagement as June broke, but was undertaken at greater range and with little damage to the Grand Fleet. But in the confusion two British cruisers were isolated and subjected to deadly gunfire from a number of German ships. One blew up immediately, the second, HMS *Warrior*, although badly damaged, was temporarily reprieved by a more tempting target, the battleship *Warspite* suffering a jammed rudder which made her turn circles in front of the German guns. (She survived to fight in World War Two, then survived that.)

Meanwhile, *Engadine* was able to take off 675 officers and men from the *Warrior*, landing them safely at Rosyth the following morning. There was no doubt that *Engadine* was in the 'front line' of the Battle of Jutland, certainly on 31st May, but when Field Marshal Haig wrote a letter of appreciation to the South Eastern board at the end of the war, it was to thank the company for its logistical work in supplying the armed forces in France. He was obviously unaware of the participation of the comparatively tiny railway steamer in the battle order of the greatest armada the world has ever seen. In contrast, the *Campania*, ten times the displacement of the SECR ship, failed to provide the Grand Fleet with scouting potential when it was crucially required. An unfulfilled naval career ended six days before the Armistice after she dragged her anchors during a storm in the Forth and collided with at least two ironclads, sinking, fortunately without casualties.

But railway steamers had no need to sail into war zones; war could just as easily come to them. The first casualty of 1916 was the *Leicester*, one of two steel Humber-built vessels introduced by the former Manchester, Sheffield & Lincolnshire Railway (later Great Central) in 1891. Well away from her usual Baltic run, she was mined in

An unusual view of a famous ship. The fate of the Great Eastern's Brussels
*is dealt with in the text, but the Dundee-built vessel is seen here aground
at Felixstowe, probably around 1907. She survived this grounding
and her sinking at Zeebrugge in 1918, ending her career
as a livestock carrier in the Irish Sea.*

(Courtesy: John Alsop collection)

the English Channel in February 1916, one of her lost crew members being Charles Larson, all of fifteen years old. Her sister ship, *Lutterworth,* was to survive the war. A fortnight later, the tender *Au Revoir* was lost. She had formerly been the *Calais,* built twenty years earlier by the South Eastern & Chatham and sold in 1911 to a Boulogne owner.

Two Great Eastern ships met misfortune at sea in 1916. The more famous of these was the *Brussels* and her story was one of the most extraordinary in the war at sea. We have already seen that the Great Eastern found itself having to increase civilian sailings to Dutch and Belgian ports after access to the Continent was no longer possible through the Baltic. The company had to charter from other railways, particularly the Great Central. All these ships, while sailing under the railway's flag, nevertheless found themselves in the cockpit of war.

History has remembered Edith Cavell, the courageous nurse put to death by the Germans in World War One, but fewer people nowadays have heard of Captain Charles Fryatt. Yet he too was victim of the German war machine, despite never carrying arms. Fryatt was a master mariner employed by the Great Eastern's marine division and he is most closely associated with the company's steamer *Brussels,* although he also appears to have skippered the Great Central's *Wrexham* in 1915 when she was chartered to the Harwich sailings. (Other GCR vessels chartered by the Great Eastern during hostilities included the *Marylebone, Notts* and *Staveley,* along with four others from that company, and one from the LYR, in 1919).

On 28th March 1915, Captain Fryatt had been in charge of the *Brussels* when she was intercepted by a U-Boat, believed to be U33, near the Maas lightship in the North Sea. Challenged to stop, Fryatt did so, but suddenly ordered full steam ahead when the Germans were about to board, and his actions caused the submarine to take emergency avoiding action. His actions saved the ship and passengers from imprisonment, or at the very least having to take to the boats in the open sea, and Fryatt was later presented with an inscribed watch. The Germans, however, were outraged, believing that Fryatt had abused truce conditions and that, in any event, they could have attacked underwater without challenge in the first place. After that, if Charles Fryatt was not exactly a marked man, his ship was seen as a worthy prize.

It might have been politic for the Great Eastern company to have found the good captain another appointment within its organisation, but nothing seems to have deterred him from going back to sea. In the meantime, on 2nd April 1916, the company's Dundee-built cargo ship *Cromer* had also repulsed a U-Boat by exactly the same tactic – ramming – causing the challenging submarine to crash-dive. The *Cromer's* skipper, Captain F. F. Beeching, was awarded the Distinguished Service Cross by the Admiralty and his Chief Officer and Chief Engineers M.Ds. (Mentions in Despatches). The Great Eastern presented all three with gold watches but it is the Naval awards which catch the eye, as these were military, not civil, decorations. It seems that the British authorities recognised that even civilian captains defending themselves or their crews in a war theatre by counter-attacking were effectively acting as belligerents.

On 23rd June 1916, the *Brussels* was stopped again by enemy units, this time five torpedo boats, and taken in prize to Zeebrugge. From there the crew were sent to Ruhleben and historian Sir Martin Gilbert quotes an eyewitness who recalled Fryatt being held held there for a month before his trial began back in Bruges. Together with his chief officer, Fryatt was tried for murder by a German court martial and both were found guilty. His chief had his sentence commuted, but Fryatt was condemned to death, and was killed by firing squad on 27th July.

If the Germans had been looking for a hostile action which would stimulate British public opinion to fight on as the Somme disaster unfolded, they could hardly have found a better one. Fryatt's fate was deplored in the newspapers of the day and condemned in the House of Commons by Prime Minister Asquith, who said that the Germans would be held to account. At the end of the war, Captain Fryatt's body was brought back to the UK, a service being held for him in St. Paul's Cathedral, and he was then taken to Dovercourt, near Harwich, where he was reinterred with honour. Meanwhile the *Brussels* was held by the Germans, although not apparently commandeered. She was eventually sunk at Zeebrugge harbour by British forces on 14th October 1918, only to be raised again the following August. This remarkable vessel ended her career as the *Lady Brussels* plying the West Coast until scrapped in 1929.

The legality of Fryatt's actions in March 1915 was questioned as much by the Germans as his execution – or murder – was by the British. Fryatt, and all his brother captains, had been told (by the Admiralty) that it was their duty to counter-attack an enemy vessel if it was possible to do so, and Fryatt's action should then have entitled him to be treated as a prisoner-of-war. After all, Captain Beeching had received a military honour after his counter-attack in the previous February. But retired mercantile master Bernard Edwards has pointed out that

Brussels *once again in distress. After her capture by the German Navy in 1916 and the execution (or murder) of her master, the GER ferry appears to have remained in Belgian waters for the rest of the war. Although later raised, she was unsuitable for passenger transport and ended her career in non-railway ownership in the Irish Sea.* (John Alsop Collection)

Admiralty instructions that a civilian vessel should attempt to ram a U-Boat could easily result in *both* vessels being mortally damaged, as the bow of a ferry was hardly reinforced in the manner of warships.

But the Germans had a horror, dating back to the first week of war, of 'franc-tireurs' – combatants posing as unarmed civilians who would then take advantage of truce conditions to overcome those to whom they had supposedly surrendered. All this legal argument might have been avoided in Fryatt's case if he had not had on his person a gold watch rewarding his attack on U-33. While the Germans knew the ship, they might not have been sure of the identity of the captain and Charles Fryatt might not otherwise have died. U-33 later perished under the guns of a Q-Boat, one of only eleven to do so.

Perhaps the only honourable facet of German behaviour in this incident was that five stewardesses from the *Brussels,* including a mother and daughter, were freed at the Dutch border three months later. Told they would have to walk with their belongings for four miles to the nearest town, they refused and the enemy relented in providing rail tickets instead.

Nor was it only the North Sea which proved a killing ground for Great Eastern ships. In the Mediterranean, the company's *Clacton* was minesweeping on 3rd August when she was torpedoed by U73 and was lost. This Hull-built freighter epitomised the somewhat muddled approach to ship requisition by the Royal Navy; if the Great Eastern could reasonably have been expected to bear the brunt of travel demands to and from north western Europe south of Denmark (and including Antwerp, whose loss to the enemy could hardly have been foreseen), then this company might have been spared losing *Clacton* to minesweeping and then having to charter accordingly. Similarly, the *Copenhagen,* lost in the following year, was operating as a hospital ship at one time. The GER's *Colchester* had already been pursued by a U-boat, as related earlier. She was not to escape the enemy in 1916.

By the midsummer of that year, Great Eastern vessels had been attacked twelve times by German warships, so not surprisingly the Admiralty decided in July 1916 to introduce a convoy system for ships venturing between the Essex coastline and the Netherlands. What *is* surprising is that this was not done earlier nor, as was to

The Great Eastern's Colchester *was captured by German forces in 1916 in circumstances that were, or should have been, controversial, as the Royal Navy was supposedly escorting her. Here the ship is seen flying the German Imperial flag shortly before she was sunk by a mine.*
(Courtesy: J. Swieszkowski collection)

be shown, was it done very effectively. The convoying of traffic in the North Sea was in fact a localised policy – one which clashed with traditional Naval practice of attack rather than defence, and no full-scale convoy policy appears to have been introduced until late in the year. The Great Eastern Railway was to suffer from its extraordinary implementation.

On the evening of the 21st of September, a convoy of four ships was being 'escorted' across the North Sea to Holland by RN destroyers. Two of the civilian vessels failed to pass the North Hinder lightship by 10.00pm, so two destroyers waited for them for onward convoying into Dutch waters. Effectively, the Navy was pursuing an 'over the horizon' policy of escorting merchant vessels by sailing a parallel path but keeping out of sight, whether by night or day. By ten o'clock on this date, two of the eastbound ships had failed to arrive, one of them the Great Eastern's ferry *Colchester*. The destroyers waited, but there was no sign of the *Colchester* or the other merchant vessel. There was no wind, the sea was calm, there had been no distress calls, no signal flares.

The destroyers' crews had heard no explosions, nor seen the flash of any gunfire, but the *Colchester* and its companion ship had vanished.

Two days later, a German news agency announced that the British ship *Colchester* had been intercepted by German surface vessels and forcibly escorted to Zeebrugge. The other ship had not even sailed. Reports as to the type of German warships involved ranged from torpedo boats to cruisers; yet the ferry was supposedly being escorted by the Navy, under its new convoy policy designed to ensure the safety of civilian vessels in a war zone! Not surprisingly, the Navy now reviewed its procedures, introducing a system of what could be described as relay escorting in daylight only, the North Sea route being divided into eight sections, each patrolled by a destroyer plying at 15 knots in a zig-zag course. This was modified to close escorting as winter set in and visibility was less dependable.

There appears to have been no criticism of the Navy's failures in the *Colchester* affair. Indeed, there was no affair anyway; the Royal Navy appears not to have attracted any public comment on what can only be described as its negligence. Apart from the loss of the railway vessel, one of the vessels being 'escorted' had not been there in the first place! (One wonders what the railway crew thought as they spent the next 26 months at Ruhleben). The ship's cargo included a large number of parcels for PoWs; interestingly, contemporary journalists fully expected these to be forwarded by the captors, but it was believed that the GPO would be dismayed at the loss of the sacks containing them. The

Colchester herself was appropriated by the Germans but was sunk when minelaying off Kiel on 2nd March 1918. Although raised and returned to the UK after the war, she was fit only for scrap.

The Official History of naval operations, begun by Sir Julian Corbett and continued after his death by Henry Newbolt, gives an interesting insight into the Royal Navy's attitude to escorting civilian vessels at this time. Naval training was basically aggressive in nature, in other words officers in the Senior Service were expected to attack the enemy on sight, just as Admiral Beatty did at every opportunity. Indeed, there was an infamous case in World War Two of a naval commander being subjected to a Court of Enquiry in November 1940 because he broke off a counter-attack on Italian forces off Cape Spartivento as he had orders to protect an important convoy. Fortunately wiser counsels prevailed on that later occasion. Captain Roskill, naval historian, wrote that in World War Two "we had to re-learn the hard way many old lessons, such as the economy and effectiveness of convoy compared to hunting for enemies at sea." He added "only the belated introduction of convoy in 1917 saved us from imminent disaster."

Another victim of the Royal Navy's casual approach to escorting duties, on 24th August, was the *Duke of Albany,* one of the largest packet steamers at 2,250 tons displacement, torpedoed in the North Sea. This was well away from her usual station, which was to provide services between Fleetwood and the north of Ireland jointly for the LNWR and LYR.

Meanwhile, the Channel continued to be a danger zone. On 26th August, the South Eastern's *The Queen* was sunk in the English Channel by German destroyers. She had been the pioneer Channel ferry powered by turbines and triple screws, and her clean lines ended in an elliptical stern more characteristic of a sailing ship. Her gracefulness did not spare this Denny-built vessel and she was sunk after the crew had taken to the boats.

Her loss was entirely preventable. *The Queen* appears to have been sailing without close escort, indeed without any escort at all, yet enemy warships were working quite openly in the Channel on a night of good visiblity. Earlier in the evening, the Great Eastern's *St. Denis* had identified nearby warships as German destroyers, but as she was operating as a hospital ship, her captain did not report the sighting by radio, as this would have jeopardised his immunity from attack. Later on that evening *The Queen* was reportedly seen "with all lights blazing" at the head of a column of five destroyers. Unfortunately they were not British as was reported, but members of the German 17th Half Destroyer Flotilla. They stopped the SECR vessel three miles off the Varne lightship – in mid-Channel – and sent an officer on board *The Queen* to order her crew and passengers into the boats, then sank her by gunfire. Lloyd's listed her as being on route from Boulogne to Folkestone with mail. Her sinking halfway between France and England by surface forces reflected little credit on the British military authorities.

Next to sink that autumn, as the British Army flung itself bravely but ineffectually against German lines in the Somme valley, was the *Rievaulx Abbey,* operated by the Wilson company on behalf of the North Eastern Railway. She was mined off the Humber with two dead on 11th September.

On 9th November, the North British Railway lost its first ship. This was the *Fair Maid,* a paddler similar in design to the *Waverley* (III), although some sixteen years newer. She was requisitioned straight off the slip and adapted as a minesweeper, but unfortunately succumbed to a mine near the Cross Sands Buoy. Her sister was luckier in this war, sweeping the seas from Sheerness, Harwich and on the Belgian coast. The *Waverley* was sunk at Dunkirk in the next conflict and a new vessel ordered immediately after the war by the LNER. The *Fair Maid's* name was resurrected, curiously, by the shipping arm of the LMS, a company not usually associated with Sir Walter Scott's writings. 1916 was not such a good year for another former NBR vessel. The paddler *Stirling Castle,* sold by the railway company eight years earlier, sank off Malta after an accidental collision when minesweeping, on 26th September. A more successful NBR convert to minesweeping was the *Roslin Castle,* purchased by the Admiralty in 1908 and still paddling in naval colours (as HMS *Nimble*) 40 years later.

Miraculously, two railway vessels, both belonging to the London, Brighton & South Coast Railway, were reported to have survived torpedo attacks in the Channel in 1916, a remarkable feat for ships lacking protective plating. The first of these was the *Sussex,* which despite her name and LBSCR co-ownership, was listed by Lloyd's as French. This plucky ship was on route from Folkestone to Dieppe with general cargo when torpedoed on 24th March, but managed to beach herself just outside Boulogne. It was here, and while awaiting repair, that the *Sussex* was sketched surreptitiously by a British army officer, James McBey, who later produced an etching of the steamer without its bow. A French sentry can be seen standing guard, suggesting that McBey's description of her as a 'troopship' was perhaps more accurate than Lloyd's listing of her as conveying general cargo. Coincidentally, another vessel of the same name, a 5,600-tonner carrying meat from Australia, survived mining in the Channel on the last day of the year. She beached herself near Dunkirk, her destination, before managing to refloat herself and deliver her cargo. Another torpedo survivor in the Channel area was the LBSC's *Rouen,* a cargo vessel which had to be towed into Dieppe after a submarine attack on 28th December.

On 19th November 1916, Field Marshal Sir Douglas Haig issued an invitation to the members of the Railway Executive Committee to come to the Somme and inspect the site of the British Army's greatest bloodbath. Haig's intention was to ensure that he had sufficient railway capacity to capitalise on any retreat by the Germans, and be able to lay tracks, both 'broad' (ie standard) gauge and 60cm gauge, onwards to Berlin. Additionally, and more prosaically, the French authorities felt that Britain should provide more of its own locomotives and rolling stock to serve its existing military bases behind the Front. In fact, the Somme offensive was just to be called

off at this time and when the ten REC representatives visited the battleground on 11th December, they could have been in no doubt that building railways across No Man's Land was hardly a major priority for the British Army, even if the improvement of existing railhead communications was. On the 16th of the month, Acting Chairman Sir Herbert Walker – who had missed the trip himself because of ill-health – formally wrote and promised "to leave nothing undone to assist in overcoming your difficulties... and thus bring the war to a successful conclusion".

There is no indication in Edwin Pratt's description of this visit – and he seems to have unquestionably accepted the pressing need to lay railways across 'the destroyed zone' – of the committee's travelling arrangements to and from France. And were they aware that railway seamen were paid so much less than other members of the sea-going profession? It would take the Ministry of Shipping's intervention to give redress on the matter, and even then not until 1918.

1917

The first half of this year saw one undeniable trend at sea – an increased and increasing percentage of merchant ships failing to reach their destinations. The statistics are stark and give no concept of the amount of pain and suffering they signify. But they are an indicator of how close Germany was to winning the war without risking another Jutland-style confrontation at sea, or even having to rush the Allied wire on land.

This led to an unusually frank speech from Lloyd George. Addressing the House of Commons on 23rd February, the Prime Minister warned that the 'submarine menace' was now so serious that Britain was going to do without many imported commodities, particularly those which took up hold space on board ship, such as timber and iron ore. To emphasise his point, he announced that the French government had

placed two complete forests at the disposal of the British Army, for trench construction and maintenance, thus avoiding the need to import timber materials. His speech pointedly did not mention potential food shortages, but despite this, he earned the praise of *The Times* for "having the courage to emphasise rather than minimise the gravity of the situation". This was at a time when the authorities were in the habit of announcing one great victory after another, each one nearer than the last.

In March 1915, 34 civilian ships were lost according to Lloyds, who included allied and neutral vessels in this total. Twelve months later, the number had doubled to 69, but this was as nothing compared to the following year. In March 1917, no fewer than 366 vessels were lost, though even that total was eclipsed by April's toll of 458, approximately one-third more again. All but 33 of this April 1917 total were victims of U-Boats. By March 1918 the loss totalled only 186, four times the corresponding 1915 figure, but provided evidence that, belatedly, the Allies were beginning to give submarine warfare the attention it required. With the United States in the war, a greater range of Atlantic convoy-escorting was possible, while acoustic detection was becoming workable and depth charges more reliable. But the introduction of convoy was the crucial factor, increasing vessel safety by a factor of 120 on one Continental passage. While three railway steamers succumbed to submarine attack in the first half of 1917, none did so in the second half. Convoy could, and should, have been introduced so much earlier. The mine continued to be a deadly weapon, indiscriminate in its sinkings.

By the latter part of the war, the Admiralty was publishing a table of ship losses on a weekly basis and including 'unsuccessful attacks by submarines'. The figures appeared to combine naval losses with those of civilian vessels and also fishing boats. The sheer extent of these statistics stretches credulity, but the ratio of aborted submarine attacks to sinkings – roughly 3 to 1 in April down to 4 to 1 in October – confirms that convoying was increasing the safety of merchant ships.

No railway ship was sunk in the first eight weeks of 1917, but the North Sea continued to be a highly dangerous war theatre, and convoying policy appears to have been applied inconsistently. This might account for the destruction of the *Cito* by German destroyers when carrying freight from Hull to Rotterdam on 17th May. Formerly part-owned by the North Eastern Railway, she was not a requisitioned vessel, nor was she apparently carrying military supplies. The fact that she was sunk by surface vessel suggests that the *Cito's* captain was unable or unwilling to obey enemy orders, but the ten lives lost might have been saved if the ship had been convoyed or escorted in the first place.

Another North Sea victim was the Great Eastern Railway's *Copenhagen,* on route from Harwich to the Hook of Holland when torpedoed by UC61 eight miles from the North Hinder Light with the loss of six lives on 5th March. This 2,250-ton triple-screw turbine vessel had served as a hospital ship for a time, and was a sister to the *St. Petersburg* and *St. Denis,* both of which would be lost in the next war.

Less than a fortnight later, the Caledonian's *Duchess of Montrose* was mined near Gravelines on the French coast, when "on Admiralty business" as Lloyd's put it. She was almost certainly minesweeping, for which paddle steamers were favoured craft because of their comparatively shallow draft. The company was formally informed of its loss by letter from the Director of Sea Transport, but the board minutes record the sinking as dispassionately, and with as few details, as Lloyd's register.

More positively, emphasising that paddle steamers could excel in a minesweeping role for the Admiralty, another member of the Caledonian fleet was the *Duchess* (later *Duke*) *of Rothesay.* This 1895 vessel swept no fewer than 500 mines, assisting in the rescuing of crews from fifteen ships, and towed a damaged German airship into Margate. Her impressive war service was spoiled only by her accidental sinking by the quayside at Glasgow in June 1919, before being refloated six weeks later. She was able to rejoin the railway fleet, as did *Duchess of Argyll,* an equally hard-working 'Caley' ship – the only non-paddle steamer from that company – which undertook 655 voyages while under military orders and on two different occasions towed the *Archangel* and the *Queen Empress* when they were damaged by collisions in the Channel.

The next loss in 1917 was a major one. The *Donegal* was a particularly handsome ship with twin propellors but reciprocating engines, rather than turbines, which her owners believed were unnecessary for such a short station as Heysham to Belfast. She was owned by the Midland Railway, a company which had most of its vessels requisitioned, and her loss in the English Channel in 1917 was one of the most serious of the war. She was employed as a hospital ship crossing with wounded from Le Havre to Southampton on 17th April in company with another ambulance vessel, the larger *Lanfranc,* when both were torpedoed without warning, despite being escorted. 80 lives were lost on the Midland ship, 29 of them crew, and the number of wounded she had been conveying had been mercifully light. Around twice as many died on the French vessel, including German prisoners among the casualties. Not surprisingly, *The Times* devoted an editorial to this atrocity in its issue for 23rd April, calling for an explanation as to the ineffectiveness of the escort. The newspaper also carried an Admiralty announcement that in future all hospital ships would lose their 'distinctive markings' and would no longer show navigation lights at night. All that can be said in the Germans' favour in this matter was that a warning had been given in January of that year that hospital ships would be treated as martial if found in a war zone.

The Times pointed out that "for nearly three years, ships carrying troops have been daily crossing [the Channel] and not one has been caught by the enemy, who must have been doing his utmost to get them...", although the paper stopped short of suggesting that the hospital ships' markings and illuminations were reckless. It also became known after the war that Molkte saw no need to attack troopships when he believed the British army faced inevitable annihilation in France in 1914 anyway. Hospital ships had been painted from the outset in alignment with the Hague Convention (and would be again in World War Two). White hull with red cross amidships and yellow funnels were the 'uniform' of such ships, with all lights being displayed at night. From 1917, following these two sinkings, uniform grey paint was applied (although this would surely make them more of a target, since they could be mistaken for warships). Camouflage was actually applied on these vessels in 1918, by which time they were classed as Ambulance Carriers and were being used as troop carriers when necessary.

But as we have seen, other mercantile steamers were in fact sunk in the Channel when on military service. In the previous month, the South Eastern's *Achille Adam* was torpedoed in the Channel. Curiously, this cargo steamer was not listed among the company's losses by railway historian Edward Pratt, while Messrs. Duckworth and Langmuir state that she "left the fleet in 1919". Lloyd's records show that she was sunk by submarine 31 miles off Beachy Head on 23rd March. Later in the year, the LBSCR cargo steamer *Maine* was torpedoed while carrying ammunition out of her home port of Newhaven to France. Built in Nantes and owned by the railway's French partner, her loss is not listed in Lloyd's. Her partner *Anjou* was sunk in an adjacent area in the following year.

A vessel far from her home waters when sunk in 1917 was the *Neptune*. This was a paddler owned by the Glasgow & South Western, one of only three companies whose ship ownership did not qualify it for representation on the REC. She and her sister *Mercury* were two of the vessels requisitioned in 1915 from the company which rivalled the Caledonian and NBR in

Clyde sailings, and both of these vessels were converted for minesweeping. *Neptune,* renamed *Nepaulin* by her new masters, was unfortunate enough to be sunk by mine near Dunkirk on 20th April, but her sister survived two minings. While operating out of Harwich, *Mercury* had her stern blown off, but managed to remain afloat. Repaired, she lasted only one day before her bow was blown off! Despite these calamities, this gallant 'South West' ship survived the war, returning to civilian life in 1920 and sailing until 1933 when replaced by a ship of similar name by the LMS, and this latter vessel served in the next war. Meanwhile, the company's only non-paddle steamer, the *Atalanta,* whose turbines were supposed to be models for those of the *Lusitania* being built in the same Clydebank yard, also undertook minesweeping and survived two submarine attacks, one of which caused her to catch fire. She too was able to return to civilian life, but undertook boom defence duties in World War Two, although no longer a railway vessel by then.

Another minesweeper lost, this time irrevocably, and because of a torpedo rather than a mine, was the Great Eastern's *Newmarket,* sunk by UC38 off Kalymos in the Mediterranean. Once again, the question has to be asked why this company should have so many ships commandeered while also being expected to continue operating the vital Harwich–Hook services. With the REC now three years old, a fairer requisition policy, worked out by the companies themselves, with the Admiralty following the army's policy of dealing with a centralised body, surely could have been introduced.

One month previously, the loss of the *Cherbourg,* joint property of the London, Brighton & South Coast Railway and a French partner, proved that the mine was an ever-present enemy. This cargo vessel was lost near Boulogne on 18th June. Confirmation of how indiscriminating a mine was in destroying friend or foe was an incident just before Christmas when three British destroyers blundered into a minefield off the Dutch coast, all sinking with the loss of more than 250 crewmen.

1917 saw the ending of the Q-Ships strategy in World War One. The idea of disguising armed ships as innocent merchantmen was always likely to be penalised by any short-term success, as suggested earlier in this

narrative. This theory is confirmed in the Official History, where Henry Newbolt wrote in the final volume that "German submarine commanders became less and less inclined to close [approach] damaged steamers, and preferred in all doubtful cases to torpedo and sink them without coming to the surface." When the Admiralty reintroduced this concept in World War Two, not a single enemy submarine was accounted for by what the Official History called "a ruse which had been so well advertised between the wars" and when the US Navy experimented with the use of decoy vessels early in 1942, the American naval historian Professor Morison commented that this was "the least useful and most wasteful of all methods to fight submarines". All this was surely predictable; the best way to protect merchant shipping from the attentions of the U-Boats was through a policy of convoying or, at the very least, properly-executed escorting.

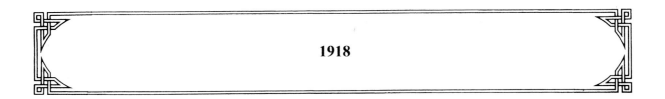

1918

The last year of World War One did not open with any sense of finality. To those on either side of the conflict, "there was" as historian Sir Martin Gilbert has recorded "no prospect of peace in Europe." Unlike 1945, there was an absence abroad of any sign that the world war might be coming to an end, of one side weakening more than another. That was, in fact, the reality, with the Central Powers unable to sustain their war effort for much longer. Yet this crumbling of resolve was undetectable to the Allies, particularly since Germany's collapse had been predicted prematurely for some time by such commanders as Douglas Haig, based on no evidence whatsoever. Indeed as the spring of 1918 opened out, so did the German assault, with the western front being almost overrun by a desperate enemy determined to try and finish the war before the Americans could arrive in large numbers.

Germany had already knocked Russia out of the war, as she had planned back in 1914, but the Allies tried to continue contact with Russian forces by shipping in supplies through the White Sea, soon to be yet another war theatre for civilian ships later in the year. Naval commanders found difficulty in liaising with the appropriate authorities as Russia turned in on herself and her struggle became internecine.

While the crews of the non-requisitioned railway steamers had to face peril in the form of destroyers, mines and submarines submerged and surfaced, just like any other merchant seamen, it was only in 1918 that a serious anomaly was addressed that had disadvantaged the railway crews. It appeared that they were seriously underpaid. In January *The Times* reported on the question of the "remuneration of seamen in cross-Channel steamers under the control of the Railway Executive Committee subject to risks not incurred by shore labour... [so] total emoluments (including war bonuses) of men on railway-owned transports and cross-Channel steamers shall be made up to an amount equivalent to the national standard rate of pay determined by the Ministry of Shipping". This inequality had clearly gone on since the first day of war some 160 weeks previously, but it appeared that the award would only be backdated as far as the previous 6th October. The new rate was equivalent to that of able seamen and firemen (stokers), namely £3 7s 6d, (£3.37½p) weekly although these employees were still expected to "find their own food".

Even if this award still appears mean-spirited considering the dangers these men had to endure, at least an injustice had finally been corrected, the newspaper commenting that the railways' previous rate had been "substantially below" that of seamen. This equalisation of pay would end with the termination of Government control less than two years later, but by that time railway pay and hours were improved considerably anyway. Nevertheless, the underpayment of railwaymen crewing merchant ships in the face of countless dangers for more than three years represented disgraceful treatment of a loyal and courageous workforce.

1918 opened with an unusual development in the war at sea and it took place in the Mediterranean. On 20th January there was a break-out from Turkish waters of the German battlecruiser *Goeben* and light cruiser *Breslau*. These two ships had enjoyed an influence on the progress of the war out of all proportion to their operational effectiveness. By sailing into the Black Sea unimpeded by the Royal Navy in 1914 they had helped convince the then-neutral Turks that Britain could not, despite its huge navy, control the high seas, and their continuing presence off Constantinople necessitated a sizeable Royal Navy presence in the eastern Mediterranean to deal with any attempt the two ships might make in combatting the Allies' Dardanelles operation. In the third week of January 1918, they made their presence doubly felt.

If the reader is wondering why this action has any relevance in the story of Britain's railway ships, the answer is that they played a remote but nevertheless significant role in the incident. When the two warships (German-officered, but flying the Turkish flag) came out from the Dardanelles, they met only light resistance and quickly sank two small Royal Naval craft. *Breslau*, however, ran into a minefield off the island of Imbros and quickly sank. Her larger companion ship had attempted to take the cruiser in tow, but further explosions made this pointless and she hurriedly left the scene but struck mines herself and, listing to 15 degrees, beached herself at Nagara Point. Here she was soon being bombed by British aircraft – something unlikely to cause an armoured ship much damage, since aerial bombing in World War One was usually carried out by hand. Within a week she was towed back to safety by a Turkish battleship and survived the rest of the war (indeed, both wars) but was no longer an operational

threat. The breakout of the two major enemy warships was hardly necessary anyway, as U-Boats operated very effectively in the Mediterranean in World War One, unaffected by a problem which would haunt them there in the second conflict – namely that they could be seen even at periscope depth from the air.

Significantly, historian Edwin Pratt insists that the mines which halted this German advance had been sown by a ship owned by the South Eastern & Chatham Railway – the *Biarritz*. Requisitioned by the Admiralty straight out of its Dumbarton shipyard in 1915, this elegant two-piper operated in home waters as a minelayer with 180 mines' capacity, before being ordered to the Mediterranean. Pratt does not reveal why he was so sure that the *Biarritz* had laid the fatal 'eggs' which accounted for the enemy vessels, but it was an operation in line with this company's notable contribution to the war at sea. A more recent historian (Brian Lavery) credits this railway minelayer as being "particularly prolific in Scottish waters", involved in the sowing of no fewer than five minefields within a year of her requisition, and all this in spite of having to store mines on her upper deck, thus threatening her stability. The official war history mentions the *Biarritz* only in connection English Channel operations and, while describing the 2,500-mine barrage laid outside the Dardanelles to deter submarines, does not name the minelayers involved. *Biarritz* herself was converted to a troop-carrier in 1919, but was to find more peaceful employment with the Southern Railway in the years between the wars. She was credited with a number of trips to the Dunkirk beach-head in the next world war and survived that too.

But the Mediterranean continued to be a deadly war zone for civilian ships supporting naval operations in 1918, and the first railway ship sunk that year was torpedoed there. She was the *Louvain*, formerly the *Dresden*, of 1897 but renamed in 1915, and used by the Admiralty as an Armed Boarding Cruiser. The death-toll was horrendous; seven officers and 217 men died, including 70 from Malta, the island's heaviest casualty list since Jutland. The *Louvain* represented yet another Great Eastern victim of the war and (arguably) of the authorities' apparent inability to requisition ships equally among the companies. Only three of the GER's ships had not been taken up by this time, according to Pratt – the *Cromer* and *Colchester*, along with the *Brussels* – and only the first of these was still usable after

P.S. "MARMION" 1906

The paddle steamer Marmion *did 'national service' in both wars, minesweeping from Dover in the first conflict and from Harwich in the second. Owned by the North British and then the LNER, this fine little paddle steamer was sunk by the Luftwaffe at Harwich in 1941.*

---

the war. The other two were both sunk while in enemy hands, although one was raised, as will be related, but did not resume her station.

Only four days later, the London & South Western lost the first of two vessels within three months and, remarkably, its first casualties in the war due to enemy action. This was the *Normandy,* a cargo vessel torpedoed eight miles outside Cherbourg when on route there from Southampton. She had been purchased in 1912 from the neighbouring LBSCR in a transaction which was uncharacteristic of railway ship owners, who tended to order from the drawing-board having specified a design which would best serve their requirements. However, as freighters, *Normandy* and her sister *Brittany* (which survived the war) were more utilitarian than passenger vessels operated by the railways and would require less company 'branding'.

The spring of 1918 saw three more railway ships torpedoed in the Channel within seven weeks, proving that the fight against the U-Boat was still not won. First to be lost was the *South Western,* the second vessel owned by the London & South Western company to

become a submarine's victim. She was in her 45th year, a veteran built in London by J. & W. Dudgeon, and sister to the *Guernsey* wrecked off the French coast because of a darkened lighthouse. Despite the tragic loss of the *South Western,* and the *Normandy* before her, this represented a remarkable safety record in such dangerous seas – Edwin Pratt believes that the LSWR company operated as many as five steamers in the Channel "every night of the week", but these two losses in early 1918 were its only losses to U-Boats.

The next U-Boat victim was the *Rye,* torpedoed on 7th April when voyaging from Newhaven in Sussex to a French port, presumably with military supplies or troops. She and her Port Glasgow-built sister *Rother* might appear to have been named after Sussex rivers, but in fact both were Lancashire & Yorkshire ships, named, in *Rye's* case, for a tributary of the Derwent in Yorkshire. Another vessel from the same company succumbed less than a month later. She was the *Unity,* torpedoed en route from Newhaven to Calais on 2nd May. Why did the authorities not notice this continuing line of casualties sailing out of the same port? Her home port would normally have been Goole and she was formerly owned by the Co-operative Wholesale Society. Also encountering a watery grave off Newhaven was another Sussex casualty in the final year of the war. This was the 770-ton cargo vessel *Anjou* whose ownership was shared between the LBSCR and its French trading partner.

Only four days later, the company's Tyne-built steamer *Hebble* was mined and sank off Sunderland. She was

51

another LYR cargo vessel named for a Yorkshire river, and she appears to have been operating commercially. Later that year, indeed only three weeks before the war ended, the company's steamer *Duke of Connaught* escaped a U-Boat by a combination of speed, and a "round or two from her defensive armament", although she was not recorded as being requisitioned and was on an Irish Sea run at the time. Less fortunate, and lost in the North Sea later that summer, was a ship which had survived not only a submarine pursuit, but attack from the air. But war was not to spare the *Kirkham Abbey*.

We have already seen that this Hull-based freighter had outrun an attacking U-Boat for twenty miles on the surface in February 1915, but she also had to survive bombing from the air off the Hook of Holland early in 1918. This was something of a precursor of what would happen to so many merchant ships in World War Two, with 'friendly fire' incidents being an added complication. Unfortunately, there was to be no escape for this hardy vessel on 27th July, torpedoed two miles off Norfolk with the loss of eight lives.

Ships were not only lost to enemy action and in the spring of 1918 it was the London & North Western Railway which lost a vessel in the kind of accident which might have been even more prevalent, with ships having to douse their lights for fear of attracting submarines or surface raiders. The 'Premier Line' ship was the *Slieve Bloom*, a Vickers-built turbine steamer introduced in 1908 for the Holyhead–Dublin service. She appears to have been operating in the Irish Sea without lights after dark when she collided with an American cruiser on 30th March 1918.

Meanwhile, the Arctic Circle was a new area for operations for British merchant ships taken up by the Royal Navy and it was in the White Sea that the first casualty resulted, on 19th June 1918. The Great Central's *Wrexham,* which had faced up to a German U-Boat some two years earlier, struck an uncharted rock and was wrecked. This Middlesbrough-built vessel had been bought second-hand by the railway and, of course, was chartered by the Great Eastern for ferry service at one stage of the war, as we have seen.

As if to serve a reminder that warmer waters were no friendlier, the Mediterranean sustained its deadly reputation into the final autumn of the war. On 12th September, the London & South Western ship *Sarnia* was torpedoed and sank, the third from that company to be lost in 1918. This Birkenhead-built vessel had accidentally accounted for the *Hythe* when colliding with the South Eastern ship off Gallipoli three years earlier and was now operating on the Admiralty's behalf as an Armed Boarding Cruiser – in an area where she was never likely to encounter enemy surface craft, disguised or otherwise. 'Sarnia' was the Latin name for Guernsey, and the final volume of the official naval history, while not mentioning the LSWR ship, lists two other Channel Island ferries – the *Lynn (Lynx)* and *Gazelle* of the Great Western. These were shown as operating with the Aegean squadrons of the Mediterranean Fleet and both survived the war. Another railway vessel which did not, succumbing to a Mediterranean mine, was the *Chesterfield,* a "tolerably handsome" (according to historians Duckworth and Langmuir) cargo vessel ordered shortly before the war by the Great Central Company and requisitioned immediately on completion.

One visitor to the Eastern Mediterranean in the final year of the war was the First Lord of the Admiralty, anxious to see the problems there for himself. He was none other than Sir Eric Geddes, formerly Assistant General Manager of the North Eastern Railway, and soon to become the first Minister of Transport and architect of the railway grouping of 1923. Somehow his presence there seemed to personify the surprisingly prominent role of Britain's railway ships in the war intended to end all wars.

The South Eastern & Chatham Railway may have regarded itself as primarily a passenger line, but with the war entering into a seemingly-endless stalemate on the Continent, the company's railways began to bear the brunt of supplying the Army on the Western Front. So intensive did this traffic become that from 29th November 1915 the Folkestone–Boulogne passage had to be barred to civilian traffic and the military given exclusive use of the station only a fortnight after the terrible accident to the *Anglia*. Even this prioritisation was insufficient to meet the military's needs and the authorities decided to create a new port on the Kent coast at Richborough, near Sandwich. Not fully functional until early 1917, this new harbour made a telling contribution to the logistics of supplying a permanent British Army on the Continent. Significantly, the port came to be associated with two transport innovations. While there had been train ferries in the UK before – from as early as the 1840s and the concept of loading and unloading trains on and off vessels with rail-equipped decks was common overseas – it was untried in cross-Channel crossings. Three such ferries were delivered for service at Richborough, with trains transferring to and from the vessels by inclined steel ramps. These ships were unimaginatively-named *Train Ferry* Nos.1-3, and were described by authors Duckworth and Langmuir as "hideous". These gentlemen were gracious enough, however, to admit they were "most useful ships". By 1924 the Tyne-built trio was put to work on the Harwich station, being taken over by the LNER, and all three served in the second conflict. We will meet them again, although two of them will be charmingly renamed as *Princess Iris* and *Daffodil*, by the Admiralty, of all people.

Train ferries were not the only traffic to be dealt with at Richborough. It was decided that instead of loading and unloading ships, which required deeper berths, and were easily detected by submarines, sea-going barges would provide a better means of transporting *materiel*. They would, of course, have the advantage of being able to penetrate the continental canal system, thus reaching inland depots supplying the military. Ideally, they should also be able to operate in the English canal network but of course that was less straightforward. This point was addressed in a letter written by Sir Herbert Walker on 7th December 1916. Writing as Acting Chairman, Walker told the Secretary of the Ministry of Munitions that "We think the time has come when the Ministry of Munitions should take in hand the question of the better use of canals throughout the country for the transport of raw materials used in the manufacture of munitions of war." In particular, Walker proposed that it should be possible to transport ordnance from the "filling factories" to the sea ports, to be met by sea-going barges "capable of negotiating the canals in France [but] it will not be possible for the self-same barges to work over the canals in this country". At least half this transport solution could be achieved through transporting ammunition etc to Richborough, loading there and taking it across the Channel.

The success of the initiative to construct an entirely new port can be surmised from the statistics. In 22 months, no less than 1.28 million tons of material were despatched to the Continent in barges, nearly one million tons of which was taken to internal canal depots. This was in addition to rail cargoes, so it is surprising to see Kentish railway author Patrick Ransome-Wallis dismiss Richborough as a wartime white elephant. The site was used in World War Two for Mulberry (floating harbour) construction, but its long-term significance lay in its proof that a custom-built facility could scarcely be bettered in meeting challenging wartime logistical problems. Of course, it is arguable that if Britain had boasted a more versatile waterways system, Richborough might not have been necessary.

Still in Kent, an unusual incident befell the South Eastern's ferry *Onward* on 24th September of that final year of war. This Dumbarton-built vessel was in Folkestone harbour when she caught fire. So serious was the blaze that the wooden supports of the quayside also caught alight, and the only means of controlling the growing conflagration was through the somewhat Pyrrhic action of opening the sea cocks and sinking *Onward* at her berth. This succeeded in putting out the flames, but no fewer than four of the company's locomotives had to be harnessed to pull her above the waterline once again. They built them sturdily on Clydeside, however, and she went 'onward' for another 29 years of service, most of it with the Isle of Man Steam Packet Company.

The Great Eastern's steamer *Brussels* left our story in May 1916. She had been taken to Zeebrugge as a prize, and her unfortunate captain later put to death, as recounted earlier. What happened to her in German hands seem unclear, although she probably remained in enemy-held Belgian waters and Lloyd's recorded that she was sunk by a British torpedo on 14th October. Raised again, she was presented to the British government by the Belgians and later was auctioned on the Tyne. Reconditioned by Henry Robb's, she became a livestock carrier in the Irish Sea before being withdrawn in 1921. The guns fell silent on the Western Front on 11th November 1918, at eleven hours on the eleventh day of the eleventh month. They fell silent at sea also, with the German High Seas Fleet being humiliatingly taken to Rosyth. (Most of the ships later scuttled themselves at Scapa Flow.) But the work of the minesweepers went on...

The Caledonian's paddle-steamers had been used for this   dangerous job, two of them perishing in the task. Of five remaining in Naval service, only one was returned to its owners within six months of the war ending; indeed one which had been being used for patrolling was now converted to minesweeping. Curiously, one author (J. A. B. Hamilton) recalled his pleasure at seeing what he described as the entire Clyde paddle-steamer fleet back in their own colours as soon after the war as August 1919. He must have included G&SWR and NBR vessels in this, however, as the official lists show an extended tour of duty for the 'Caley' boats. As for their North British rivals, the paddlers *Edinburgh Castle* and *Lord Morton* were taken up in the spring of 1918, although they were configured as ambulance carriers for the White Sea, an area where minesweeping was not so crucial. Both were blown up by the Royal Navy in the following year, when it became obvious that the Bolsheviks (Communists), in becoming the dominant force in Russia, were about to requisition the former NBR ships – a sad end for two vessels well-loved on the Firth of Forth. (Strictly speaking, these had been operated by the Galloway Saloon SP Company, in which the North British held a majority interest.)

Two other vessels to perish after the war's end were still involved in the deadly matter of minesweeping. One was the *Mars*, a G&SWR paddler operated by the Navy as HMS *Marsa*. Exactly one week after the Armistice, she was run down by a destroyer while carrying out her minesweeping duties outside Harwich on 18th

The Waverley *is the last ocean-going paddle steamer in the world and this is her immediate predecessor, the third of that name. Delivered in 1899, the vessel is seen here in her World War One garb, with her bridge behind the funnel. This fine NBR and LNER ship served in both wars, failing to survive the second in tragic circumstances. Offered the chance to leave Dunkirk under the protection of an anti-aircraft cruiser in May 1940, her captain instead turned back to assist an LMS paddler and thus mortally exposed the ship to the wrath of the Luftwaffe.*

November. Although her crew managed to partially beach her, she proved beyond help and soon broke in two. It was tragic that she should survive the highly-dangerous trade of drawing the sea's explosive sting only to succumb to a night-time collision with a friendly vessel. Farther afield, and even later after the war's end, the Solent paddler *Duchess of Richmond* was blown up by mine in the blue waters of the Aegean on 28th June 1919. She was probably the last ship victim of the enemy in World War One, certainly among the railway steamers.

Postscript to World War One

Field Marshal Earl Haig's letter of 1918 to the South Eastern & Chatham Railway has already been mentioned in this book's coverage of the First World War, but it is worth looking at again as it encapsulated what many military personnel, high and low, must have felt about the contribution made by the railways in both World Wars in the twentieth century.

"Track has been torn up to give us rails; engines, trucks, men, capable operating staff etc., all have been sent abroad to us, regardless of the special needs and demands of the people at Home, and without any hesitation."

As head of the armed forces on the Continent, Haig only assessed the railways' contribution in terms of supply of materials and staff, so he can perhaps be forgiven for what was a somewhat limited perspective of the railways' work. For nowhere in his letter of 23rd December 1918 did he mention the contribution of the railway ships. Whether taken up by the Royal Navy, or left to sail on reduced or altered civilian services, railway vessels played a vital part in the Allied victory.

Under the White Ensign, paddle steamers swept mines and ferried troops in and out of danger areas from Dunkirk to Archangel, former channel steamers took wounded servicemen home through submarine-infested seas. Even if not requisitioned, railway ships plied through waters where U-boat commanders had sworn to sink all British ships on sight, and where even a 'friendly' mine could slip its 'sinker' and threaten any passing hull. But some company steamers did even more than this. The involvement of the *Engadine* at Jutland – the only non-armoured ship on either side – was the height of achievement for a requisitioned civilian ship, and belonged to the very company whose contribution was assessed by Haig purely in logistical terms.

To be fair to Haig he was exclusively writing on behalf of the Army, but his omission of any mention of the ships' and crews' role sums up the neglect of their contribution. The authorities of the day, not to mention subsequent historians, have underrated, or even been unaware of, the service and sacrifice made by railway companies and their ship crews in the battle to maintain supremacy of the sea and to ensure that troops and supplies reached their destinations. The SECR alone transported 3.5 million personnel across the Channel without a single loss. This is in addition to the initial transport of the BEF, to say nothing of the participation of railway ships in minelaying and sweeping.

If Haig was unaware of this contribution, we should not be.

Britain entered World War Two on 3rd September 1939, but for civilian shipping its effects were felt earlier. Just as in the first conflict, when the Admiralty dealt directly with owners of ships which it wished to requisition, so in the second, there was no delay in the STUFT process. Control of all British merchant shipping was adopted on 26th August by the Admiralty's Trade Division, although actual procurement of ships required was soon to be the province of the Ministry of Shipping, re-established by the following October. Thus was a lesson learned from World War One, when responsibility for ship requisition was at first too simple, and later in the conflict too complicated, especially when insurance claims had to be met for losses at sea. In May 1941 the new shipping Ministry merged with the Ministry of Transport to form the Ministry of War Transport.

As in the first conflict, a railway company owning ships – and that was all four of the main line companies – would find itself approached by letter regarding their requisition. From October 1939 onwards, this document, marked secret, came from the Superintending Sea Transport Officer of the Ministry of Transport. Each letter economically used Board of Trade stationery, with the advice that if the Board's name had not been crossed out anywhere in the document, it should be read as 'Ministry of Shipping' (paper was of course an increasingly valuable commodity at the time).

The last Great Eastern ship to be introduced on to the Harwich station was the Tyne-built Malines. *She is seen here in company colours not long after completion in 1921 but she spent most her working life as a LNER vessel. She had a varied war career, being present at Dunkirk, but was torpedoed from the air in the Mediterranean in 1942. Although subsequently raised, she served mainly as a dockside depot ship.*

The letter opened with a stirring appeal: "His Majesty's Government relies on the goodwill of yourselves, your staff and agents, in carrying out these instructions and preparing the ship for the King's service, especially as regards clearing cargo, fuelling, stowing, and manning'. It went on to explain the formal wording under which requisition would take place – Charter Party T98. This was "a net form of charter under which His Majesty's Government takes all marine and war risks, is liable for all running expenses of the ship, crew, and stores, undertakes to restore the craft, her outfit and machinery to the Owners in the same condition as when taken over, ordinary wear and tear and depreciation alone excepted. To assist the Government in the preparation of the craft for sea, Owners may, however, be required to undertake certain services in connection with the craft, on a repayment basis."

Information required by the Navy had to be filled in on an accompanying form, including questions which now appear incredibly dated. Was fuel solid or oil? If oil, was this to fuel steam or Diesel propulsion? If solid, what quantity was in the ship's bunker at that time?

Details of construction cost and present insurance cover were also requested. There were one or two curious conditions. While there appeared to be no requirement that the crew should be British – perhaps this was taken as read – any temporary crewmen involved in moving the ship to the dock where the Navy would take over were required to be British subjects (there was no nonsense about 'citizens' in those days!). Also curious was a rule that no Member of Parliament could be involved in any chartering contract – doubtless to avoid any conflict of interest - yet members of the House of Lords (part of Parliament) could be found in almost every railway boardroom.

Although not specified in the document, it became normal practice for the crew to be 'taken up' at the same time as the vessel, although this does not appear to have been mandatory. Crewmen remained merchant seamen, although they came under Naval discipline, their masters and chief engineers being offered commissions in the Royal Naval Reserve. Crews were assured of insurance against 'war risks', although the first conflict had shown that ships could be wrecked because of a

Vidière éditeur - Dieppe

A commercial postcard showing an accidental grounding of the Newhaven *in August 1924. Originally an LBSCR steamer, she was later registered as French. Many English-based vessels carried the names of Continental ports and cities and this ship's sister was the* Rouen.

darkened lighthouse (*Guernsey*) or an underwater rock in an area not properly charted (*Wrexham*), and these were borderline cases where lawyers or insurance assessors might have to be brought in. While more bureaucratic than the requisition process in World War One – although still amazingly light in terms of today's paperwork – railway officials in World War Two were not slow in answering their country's call.

This author has examined requisition papers received by the LNER by the afternoon post at 4.45pm, one day in May 1940. The ship was handed over before lunch the next day.

In 1941 the Government issued what appears to have been an unnecessary piece of legislation relating to ship requisition, the Use and Hire of Ships Control Order, which came into effect on 22nd May of that year. This decreed that no ship of more than 1,600 tons gross could be hired without Government approval. In World War One the Great Eastern had chartered from the Great Central, and the latter from the North Eastern, but any interchanging among the railway companies in the second conflict (which does not appear to have happened) would have been overseen by the Railway Executive, so much more professionally-organised than in its World War One guise, and effectively an arm of Government anyway. An interesting aside on the 1941 order appeared in *The Times* the day before it came into effect. The newspaper's shipping correspondent pointed out that "as all British ships of more than 1,600 tons gross are now either requisitioned by, or licensed to, the Ministry of War Transport, it follows that the new Order relates to vessels owned outside this Country."

If shipping journalists were surprised at the issuing of this Order, the historian can only perceive it as touching on railway steamers where ownership was shared between the Southern Railway and French concerns,

The Great Western Railway was rightly proud of the courage shown by its seamen, never more so when two of its freighters, the Roebuck *and* Sambur, *approached St. Valery to rescue British troops in June 1940 without a promised naval escort and in a location where a LNER ferry had already been destroyed. Here the latter ship is seen on a more peaceful occasion.*

both commercial and nationalised. Since jointly-owned vessels such as *Rouen* had performed heroically at Dunkirk, and with no suggestion of anything less than full dedication to the Allied cause, it would appear that this outburst of red tape was prompted by little more than the Ministry of Shipping's disappearance into the Ministry of War Transport in that very month.

In comparing the service of railway ships in two world wars, it is immediately obvious that there were fewer seas for them to ply. For four years from June 1940 the whole European seaboard from North Cape almost as far south as Spain was occupied by the Nazi enemy, with complete air superiority for most of that time. With the Germans occupying (from north to south) Norway, Denmark, the Netherlands, Belgium and northern France, there was no question of cross-Channel ferrying as happened throughout the first conflict. Even north-south coastal shipping off Britain's east coast was subject to attack from U-Boat, aircraft and fast-moving E-Boats, the last being a type of torpedo boat whose challenge the Royal Navy struggled to contain.

From the summer of 1940, when France was overcome and Italy promptly joined the war, the Mediterranean in turn became almost impassible. Even the mightiest of British warships struggled to make the passage between Gibraltar and Alexandria, menaced by U-Boats, while the Italian Air Force, supplemented by the Luftwaffe, exerted air superiority – all this accounting for a veritable fleet of British capital ship victims within eighteen months. One aircraft carrier was sunk (*Ark Royal*), and two badly damaged (*Illustrious, Formidable*), one battleship sunk (*Barham*), two disabled (*Queen Elizabeth, Valiant*), and one other heavily damaged (*Warspite*), all in the Mediterranean in 1941. And that is before the battle for Crete is considered, when heavy cruiser and destroyer losses were sustained.

The memory of LNWR, Great Central and LSWR steamers plying the Mediterranean, challenging suspect vessels and ferrying troops, was one that was never to be repeated, certainly not on such a scale. Once air superiority had been established later in the second conflict, a number of railway ships were able to sail in Mussolini's 'Mare nostrum', although with varying fates – the Great Western's *St. David* was lost at Anzio and the LNER's *Malines* sunk, and then raised again, off Egypt. Additionally, vast ocean waters of the Atlantic, Arctic and Pacific provided the backdrop for this war and, needless to say, railway ships were also involved in these theatres.

There is no official volume exclusively covering naval operations in World War Two, similar to the Official History of such operations in the previous conflict which was published over a ten-year period up to 1931. While its disappointing marginalising of requisitioned and mercantile steamers has been commented upon already, the five-volume *Naval Operations [in the Great War]* (see bibliography) was at least a voluminous and readable account of the war at sea from 1914 to 1919.

In contrast, a similar approach in publishing a history of World War Two at sea would have in turn marginalised the work of, for example, the RAF Coastal Command, and perhaps also have led to a fragmented account of amphibious operations. "My charter is to tell the story of the maritime war in all its aspects" wrote Captain Stephen Roskill in his introduction to *The War at Sea 1939-1945,* whose first volume was published by Her Majesty's Stationery Office in 1954. Captain Roskill seemed reluctant to name railway and other commercial vessels in his narrative, but in many cases he simply had to – such successful operations as Dynamo (Dunkirk 1940) and Overlord (D-Day, 1944) would not have succeeded without them. In the rest of this narrative, where your author refers to 'the Official History', this is the work intended. Roskill's work was checked by the Churchill administration before publication of the first volume in 1954. According to David Reynolds in his recent book *In Command of History,* the Prime Minister could not be persuaded to accept Roskill's account of the losses of December 1941 – of the capital ships *Prince of Wales* and *Repulse* – without the help of "two or three double brandies". An accurate and officially-approved history then, but not written to flatter those in power.

When we read in its pages that, on one visit to Dunkirk in 1940, the *Whippingham* of the Southern Railway took off 2,700 troops and the same company's *Maid of Orleans* 1,856 – 50% more than three naval destroyers taking part at the same time – it is difficult to avoid the conclusion that railway and other commercial ships played just as important a role in the Second World War as they had in the First, and railways, in making some 120 vessels available to the military, in some cases at a few hours' notice, had played their part to the full.

Unfortunately Roskill failed to mention some of the typical acts of gallantry from railway ships' masters and crews during such operations as Dynamo; indeed, his mention of such losses is usually cryptic, with no allowance for the fact that he was describing vessels whose crews had volunteered to put themselves in harm's way in thin-skinned ships, often lightly armed. The scorning of the German guns by the LNER's ferry *Malines* in escaping from Dutch waters, the same company's *Waverley* turning back at Dunkirk to help a stricken ship while Stukas wheeled above, the GWR captain who refused to turn back from evacuating a French harbour when the local pilot declined to assist, and the Southern ship which cast off, then reberthed, when abandoned soldiers ran for their lives along the quay towards it... that there is no official history of such courage and selflessness is a sad comment on how little railway crews have been credited in this war.

The requisitioning of civilian vessels at the start of World War Two has already been described. The Ministry of Shipping was established as soon as possible after the declaration of war, but however requisitioning proceeded, one of the first tasks of the Navy's Trade Division in 1939 was to organise defensive arming of the Merchant Navy. The earliest weapons to be fitted were salvaged from scrapped warships, but the availability of anti-aircraft weapons, new or second-hand, was at a premium, and was to prove a chronic problem for requisitioned vessels (and for the fighting ships as well). Typical weaponry for a pleasure paddle steamer being taken up would be a 12-pounder on her bows, requiring a guncrew no fewer than eight men strong. Lighter Lewis armaments were installed on each paddle box. Even more ordnance was added when some of the steamers joined the anti-aircraft defences of London from 1941 onwards, now also packing rocket launchers and multiple machine guns. Crew training in the use of weapons involved some 150,000 crewmen, but was never as effective as it might have been, as will be shown. In addition, the problems of aircraft recognition were never fully resolved, and were equally bad in the Royal Navy, resulting in an unfortunate number of 'friendly fire' incidents when ships' crews cheerfully blazed away at any passing RAF plane. Of course, it was not unknown for British aircraft to attack British ships!

"Duchness of Rothesay"

Paddle steamers had shown themselves to be ideal for minesweeping in the previous war, with their shallow draft permitting close inshore working. Additionally, their stability allowed for two sweeps to be operated simultaneously by each vessel, once Oropesa equipment was adopted in World War Two. By 1940, no fewer than 30 paddlers, mostly of railway origin, had been taken up for minesweeping by the Royal Navy. They operated initially in five flotillas:

    7th Flotilla, seven vessels based Granton, on the Forth
    8th, five at North Shields, on the Tyne
    10th, eight at Dover
    11th, five at Greenock, on the Clyde
    12th, five at Harwich.

These formations did not last the duration; the Granton flotilla was the longest-serving, remaining on station until 1943. (Incidentally, a Mass Observation correspondent working in a shipping office recorded the staff's dismay at the company losing its overseas markets at the onset of war, to be replaced by relief at unexpectedly gaining a Government contract 'to bunker minesweepers at Granton'.) By 1943 most of the improvised minesweepers (those which survived) were being converted for other duties. Of the five flotillas above, the 11th was the only local formation, based on

With a working history of 50 years, PS Duchess of Rothesay *of the Caledonian and LMS Railways was one of the most celebrated of Clyde steamers, known as 'Cock of the Walk' from a small weather-cock fixed to her mast. In the second conflict, she replaced the doomed* Waverley *in the Harwich minesweeping flotilla in 1940. After that, her cruising days were over, but her war record had been second to none.*

Clyde ships alone, although made up of rival LMS and LNER steamers. The other groups were more cosmopolitan, exhibiting the military mind's usual habit of stationing men and machines as far away as possible from their home areas – it is no surprise that one Scottish steamer's – the *Kylemore's* – short World War Two career involved service at Dover and then, fatally, at Harwich, while Portsmouth paddlers such as the *Ryde* and *Sandown* operated from Granton and their crews had to hastily familiarise themselves with the east coast from the Tay to the Farne Islands. The latter was never to return south, mined off the Tyne, while, astonishingly, the former still exists, awaiting scrapping at time of writing.

Sweeping equipment consisted of Oropesa apparatus comprising cutting cables suspended from torpedo-shaped floats (now called paravanes), the idea being to snag and cut the mine's mooring cable, thus forcing it to the surface where it could be dealt with by gunfire, sometimes even just rifle fire. Oropesa equipment – named after the trawler from which it was first tested by the Admiralty – allowed sweeping to be carried out by one vessel at a time, an improvement on World War One methods.

In 1940 a Government-approved book by A. D. Divine, entitled *Behind the Fleets,* gave the reading public a surprising amount of detail of minesweeping methods: "A wire is dropped over the stern, [and] fast to the end of it is a trawl door or a vaned steel kite. With the paddle-steamers two wires are used, one over each quarter, and with the dragging of the kites they work out in a great quarter circle on either hand. And to mark their passage, and to keep constant depth, there is above each kite a float, shaped like a torpedo and painted grey – painted grey save above the nose."

One pleasure steamer whose short military career in this new war summed up the pathos and problems of her kind when requisitioned for minesweeping was the *Kylemore.* She was a 42-year old paddler and veteran of World War One operations, owned by the Caledonian Steam Packet Company, controlled by the LMS. Not long after the declaration of war, this venerable steamer was given a hurried conversion, guns bolted on, windows boarded over, her bright paint obscured with grey, and she left Troon harbour to a farewell chorus of ships' hooters and sirens in December 1939. She was never to return.

Ordered to the south coast to join the 10th Minesweeping Flotilla working out of Dover, Captain Fergus Murdoch and his crew discovered that theirs was

Like a number of railway ferries in the first war, the Southern Railway's Invicta *was requisitioned straight from the shipyard in 1940, but not assigned a role as a landing ship until two years later. She made up for lost time in August 1942 by taking part in the Dieppe Raid, landing Canadian troops and sustaining damage in a disastrous attack on the German-held coast. Her later, more peaceful, career began with cross-Channel services in 1946.*

the slowest ship in the formation, so naturally they were given the job of destroying the mines swept by the vessels in column ahead. In 1940 the readers of *Behind the Fleets* were given a fairly detailed description of a typical mine's destruction: "Out there on our starboard quarter we saw the float stagger and dip, and then give back again. Then suddenly we felt the wire ease, and with a shattering of spray, with a great blackness in that wave of white, the mine shot clear to the surface and fell back wallowing in the spume. There was a cheer below us on the deck; there was a scramble for the machine-gun, for rifles. The sea was suddenly alive with the brisk staccato stabbing of the shots. We heard come back from that dark shape that wallowed, the clanging of the hits, and then, suddenly, we saw bright flame and leaping water, and the enormous uprush of the burst."

Unfortunately, the crew of *Kylemore* had been given no proper artillery training and no opportunity to practice using their 12-pounder. Not surprisingly, they erratically expended no fewer than 50 shells on their first mine, a contact ordnance whose prongs had to be struck. For this, the *Kylemore's* crew were ragged unmercifully by the rest of the flotilla! Perhaps this was not unconnected with her conversion to net-laying shortly afterwards. But whatever her function, she was important enough to be targeted successfully by the Luftwaffe at Harwich on 21st August 1940.

Within the first year of war, the authorities realised that minesweepers needed to be more sophisticated than in the previous conflict. This was because of the introduction of 'influence' mines. The first railway steamer to succumb in World War Two in fact fell victim to a magnetic device; the former Lancashire & Yorkshire, now LMS, cargo vessel *Mersey* was sunk in this way in the Channel on St. George's Day in 1940. To quote Mr. Divine again: "Mr. Churchill, towards the end of February [1940], said that the story of the conquest of the magnetic mine was 'a detective story written in a language of its own'. Mr. Churchill erred on the side of understatement."

Magnetic mines necessitated sweeper vessels with hulls wholly or partly constructed of wood, while paddle steamers, so dependable in this role in World War One, were, with their threshing wheels, hardly the most suitable vessels to tackle acoustic or barometric mines. Within three years, more paddle steamers (nine) had been lost sweeping than were still in service (six) undertaking this hazardous work, according to *The War at Sea*, Vol. II. On the other hand, such vessels had an obvious use as short-distance troop carriers as we shall see. Even one steamer with as little as 250 tons displacement when empty, and licensed to accommodate 540 passengers and crew on a pleasure trip, would carry enough life-saving gear (lifeboats, lifebuoys and what the Board of Trade defined as 'buoyant apparatus') to save over 1,300 individuals. At Dunkirk, one paddle steamer took off twice as many troops as that!

Gradually, those paddle-minesweepers which survived the first eighteen months of war would be found less perilous jobs as mine technology demanded increasingly sophisticated countermeasures, rendering these older vessels redundant. Paddlers found new roles, such as netlayers or anti-aircraft vessels. Table IV summarises and illustrates this progression, listing only those railway paddle steamers which survived their first, (usually) minesweeping, role. As mentioned above, by February 1942, the Admiralty had decided to provide mobile anti-aircraft batteries to help protect London by deploying twelve paddle-steamers in the Thames estuary. These bristled with two 2 single 2 x pounder A/A guns, two Lewis guns, no fewer than twelve

machine guns in quadruple turrets, as well as two four-barrel rocket launchers. Designated as Thames Special Service Ships, they were known familiarly (and even to Captain Roskill, author of the Official History) as 'Eagle Ships' after their two most famous members, the local excursion paddlers *Royal Eagle* and *Golden Eagle*. The latter had rescued survivors from the doomed *Waverley* at Dunkirk, on the day when her Thames sister *Crested Eagle* was lost. These were of course non-railway vessels, but as Table IV shows, no fewer than eight railway-owned paddle-steamers underwent conversion to A/A ships, one, the LMS's *Juno*, being bombed and lost during this work. Roskill comments in Vol. I of the *The War at Sea* that "their manouevrability, and the good gun platforms obtained from their wide beam, made them very suitable for this class of work".

Hospital ships, or Ambulance Carriers, had been an essential part of the auxiliary fleet in World War One, ferrying the wounded from the Continent to British ports whence they could be taken inland by ambulance train for treatment. That was the theory anyway, but the reality was that battlefield wounds were usually contaminated by dirt from soldiers' uniforms, all too frequently leading to death from septicaemia or other forms of blood poisoning. One surgeon working at an army hospital in France, and dismayed by medicine's failure to combat this contamination with any kind of effective antibiotic, was a certain Alexander Fleming. Nevertheless, great store was set on bringing casualties back for hospital treatment whenever possible, and we have already seen that many railways found their larger ships being requisitioned for this purpose.

In the second war, such ferrying was unlikely to be required from 1940 until the Second Front was established, although that could hardly have been anticipated, with again a number of rail ships being modified as hospital vessels. Of eight hospital ships used in Operation Dynamo in 1940, all were from the railways, five of them from the Southern, three from the GWR 'Modified' is an adverb which itself requires qualification. Little alteration was carried out except replacing furnishing with camp beds, and the operating equipment was limited. Not surprisingly, a number of these vessels saw use in support of the D-Day landings, firstly as administrative or reserve ships, then reverting to their hospital role.

Winston Churchill began World War Two as First Lord of the Admiralty and, from May 1940, assumed the taxing role of Prime Minister. In this shot he is seen visiting the Home Fleet at Scapa Flow on board what appears to be a GWR tender vessel usually employed at Plymouth. The Great Western's tenders were the first railway ships to be requisitioned in the first war and among the first in the second, giving sterling service throughout both conflicts.

Despite its name, the Southern's *Autocarrier,* with deck capacity for 35 cars, required vehicles to be loaded and unloaded by crane. This did not preclude her from a vigorous naval career, however, and she received a favourable mention from Captain Roskill for her role at Dunkirk, where she took part in the evacuation of 3rd and 4th June, with German forces only three miles from the town.

Train ferries, although numbering only six in 1939, were worth their displacement in gold, their flat decks with open sterns ideal for storing and laying mines. The three 'hideous' rail vessels from the Richborough station in World War One were operating out of Harwich by 1939, but their 60 feet-wide decks offered considerable operational scope. Little wonder that the Admiralty, with

unusual sentimentality, sought to find them more euphonious names to carry during their military service (*Princess Iris, Princess Daffodil*) and the former features in the Official History. Two of the three failed to survive the war. That the conversion of such specialised vessels for minelaying duties began immediately on the outbreak of war is indicated by the Official History's comment that the conveyance of the BEF's supplies to France was slowed by two of the train ferries' being adapted for their new role. This refers to the Southern Railway ferries *Hampton Ferry* and *Shepperton Ferry,* engaged in minelaying outside Dover and Folkestone within a week of war being declared, although there would appear to be an immediate demand for their services in their designed role. The Southern ferries would have been doubly useful, conveying up to 30 road vehicles as well as ten Continental-length rail wagons or carriages.

This kind of wide-deck facility was also offered by road vehicle ferries, particularly if an open stern was available for sowing. One such vessel involved in laying minefields was the *Princess Victoria*, also mentioned in Roskill's history. This ferry was involved in creating a North Sea mine barrier, largely completed by May 1940. Unfortunately, the *Princess* was not to complete her commission, as will be related. Not all vehicle ferries, were configured for 'drive-on, drive-off' operations.

When returned to their real purpose of rail ferrying, the three Southern Railway train ferries were involved in heavy logistical operations once the Allies had re-entered Europe in 1944. This is a peacetime shot of Twickenham Ferry; *huge gantries capable of lifting and loading 'Austerity' locomotives were fitted to their sterns towards the end of the war. The SR vessels were luckier than their LNER counterparts, two out of three of which were lost.*

LEFT
Two of the three LNER train ferries operating on the Harwich station failed to survive World War Two. Train Ferry No.3, *seen here in peaceful days, was renamed* HMS Daffodil *but was the last railway vessel to be mined, in the Channel in March 1945, and some reports say she took a cargo of locomotives to the seabed.*

Just as in 1914, one of the first naval operations was the transport of a British Expeditionary Force to the Continent. An additional burden was the supplying of materials for the Advanced Air Striking Force, although the planes themselves would of course fly to whatever base was selected inland. Destroyers were used to carry advance parties of military personnel to Cherbourg from as early as 4th September, just 24 hours after the declaration of war; it was decided early during this operation that no French ports east of Le Havre would be used, except for the ferrying of rail vehicles by at least one train ferry. This was apparently to satisfy the French authorities, who feared that the use of these ports would attract air attacks. Troops were ferried from the 9th onwards, mainly from Southampton and the Bristol Channel, although Roskill does not name the vessels involved. At least, these appear to have been escorted this time, and the entire operation was a complete success. An army of 161,000 men, with 24,000 vehicles and 140,000 tons of stores was transported. With a period known as the 'Phoney War' about to begin, there was considerable leave traffic between the Channel ports at the end of the year, a total of some 200,000 men being ferried in both directions over the winter.

The war was 'phoney' only on land; the Royal and Merchant Navies had no breathing space to enjoy. Routine duties such as minelaying and minesweeping, netlaying, boom defence construction – all these tasks had to be undertaken daily. This was in addition to supplying the BEF in Europe and military bases in the Middle and Far East. The escorting of merchant vessels was again a problem for the Royal Navy, which happily adapted to a plan for 'hunting groups' from Winston Churchill (back at the Admiralty as the new First Lord).

These groups were flotilla-sized formations of capital ships and cruisers deployed in selected areas where German commerce-raiders were believed to be active. Rather than accompanying convoys, or patrolling shipping lanes, the hunting groups appear to have scoured the seas at random during daylight – most of the hunters still being unequipped with radar. The Battle of the River Plate, in which the German 'pocket battleship' *Graf Spee* was scuttled after attack by three Commonwealth cruisers in December 1939, was a great feat of arms, but in many ways was a fluke, and no other hunting group had similar success in the first year of war. The groups, apart from fulfilling Churchill's desire to take the war to the enemy at all times, represented naval commanders' apparent reluctance to undertake close escorting of merchant ships.

The Official History (Volume II) actually quotes Admiral Tovey, commanding the Home Fleet in 1942, as saying that attempting to sink a German battleship was "of incomparably greater importance to the conduct of the war than the safety of any convoy", emphasising what Captain Roskill describes as "the tradition that the destruction of the enemy's principal forces should be the object of our fleet". To be fair to the Admiralty, it had ordered Tovey to give greater attention to convoy protection, but individual commanders clearly saw their role as undertaking Jutland-style confrontations. Yet it was a civilian liner which occupied the very first position in the war's list of ships missing and sunk. The 13,000-ton *Athenia* was torpedoed by U30 on the first day of war, 3rd September 1939.

While requisitioned ships trained and adapted for the trials ahead, and while other railway steamers – particularly the ferries – supplied the needs of the Army

Two LNER ships were lost in the Le Havre area in June 1940 when an attempt was made to rescue the 51st Highland Division. One such vessel was the former GER vessel Bruges, *sunk by gunfire although most of her crew were immediately picked up by another LNER ship, the* Vienna. *This peacetime photograph shows stern detail on the Clydebank-built vessel.*

The Duke of York *had a war almost as eventful as that of the battleship whose completion caused the LMS steamer to have her name changed to* Duke of Wellington. *However named, she had an exciting war, being present at St. Valery, Dieppe and the Normandy beaches.*

on the Continent – the first winter passed without a single loss of a railway ship to enemy action. This good fortune was not destined to last.

The month of May 1940 saw a notable railway ship loss. The *Princess Victoria* had only been completed as recently as the previous October, built by Denny to the order of the LMS. She was intended for the Stranraer–Larne run, which could have been a train-ferry service were it not for the gauge difference (Northern Ireland's railways are of course broad gauge). The vessel had a covered 'hangar' deck capable of taking heavy road vehicles, but just as importantly, with a stern-loading configuration, she was ideal for minelaying.

On 24th January 1940 she laid no fewer than 240 mines 50 miles north east of Spurn Point, on the Humber, and followed this up with dummy mines to the east of this barrier, the latter operation intended to deter enemy mining. This was considerable, with U-Boats and disguised merchantmen sowing a deadly assortment of acoustic, contact and barometric sensitive ordnance, with the Luftwaffe an additional delivery system. One of these devices may have accounted for this fine LMS vessel. Equally possible was that the agent of her destruction on 18th May was one of her own mines, as she sank off the Humber, the estuary she had worked so

hard to protect. No fewer than 36 lives were lost, including the captain, and seven of these were LMS employees. 85 survivors were landed safely later that day.

The *Princess Victoria* had just taken part in a destroyer-led operation to lay a field off the Dutch coast as a cruiser squadron entered Ijmuiden to arrange for the embarkation of the Netherlands' gold reserves and, shortly afterwards, the Dutch royal family. The LMS ferry was not the only railway vessel involved; the LNER's North Sea ferries *St. Denis* and *Malines* had both been sent to Rotterdam to evacuate British civilians at the end of May, but the former was so badly damaged by bombing that she had to be scuttled in what were rapidly becoming enemy waters. Her complement was picked up by the *Malines,* which doused its lights and slipped downriver in darkness under the barrels of the German guns. This courageous action is not mentioned in the Official History.

Defeats on land represented a closing of the noose around the United Kingdom – soon there would be no friendly coast on the European seaboard. As for the *Princess Victoria,* she was to be succeeded soon after the war by another of the same name and design, and was destined for an equally unhappy end. The loss of this new LMS ferry in May 1940 took place just days before one of the biggest-ever mobilisations of civilian ships in support of a military operation.

This was Operation Dynamo. That was what the commanders called it. The pessimists called it a disaster, the optimist a success. The men who were there had their own opinion.

Chapter 6
DUNKIRK

'Excursion into Hell' was the phrase coined by author J. B. Priestley in describing how pleasure steamers and assorted small craft answered the call to make their way into the war zone of North West France in the last days of May and the first days of June, in 1940. These were among the last days of Allied occupation of the mainland of Western Europe for more than four years, as the German forces proved irresistible in their drive westwards to the Channel. The climax of this triumphant progress in 1940 was the British army being literally driven into the sea while Belgium, then France, surrendered. From Dunkirk and a number of other ports on the Channel seaboard, the troops looked seaward for ships. They were not slow to arrive and railway ships were prominent among them.

New Prime Minister Winston Churchill hoped that 50,000 troops could be saved and felt that 100,000 would be a miraculous figure. While this was to be exceeded three times over, little in the way of heavy weapons or equipment could be brought out – a sobering thought when the reader considers Captain Roskill's report that no fewer than 89,000 vehicles had been taken to France

for the BEF's use from September 1939 onwards. No wonder Churchill cautioned a relieved nation that a retreat can hardly be considered a triumph. But a breakdown of the evacuation is worth examining, particularly in a book on railway steamers, since the nine days of Dunkirk represented a compressed example of all the heroism of these civilian crews in two world wars. For this reason, the author makes no apology for treating the Dunkirk episode in some detail.

Renamed HMS Oriole, *the LMS paddler* Eagle III *took part in the Dunkirk evacuation of 1940, with her naval commander deliberately beaching her to make it easier for soldiers to climb aboard. Unfortunately she was unable to make a quick getaway and her plight attracted the attention of the LNER's* Waverley, *which failed to refloat her and was mortally attacked herself. Despite this, the* Eagle *survived the war but required repairs which would have been uneconomic to carry out.*

The Southern Railway's paddle steamer Whippingham *made a remarkable crossing to Dunkirk on 1st June 1940. She embarked no fewer than 2,700 men – the equivalent of more than two battalions – and delivered them safely to 'Blighty', with her paddle housings only inches above the water. She survived to serve the public until 1962, while her sister* Southsea *perished in a wartime incident in 1941.*

By the third week of May 1940, it was obvious that the BEF's position in Belgium and northern France was unsustainable, and that some degree of evacuation would have to be contemplated. Ironically, this initially involved taking troops *into* France, in order to secure the perimeters of Boulogne and Calais. What the Official History calls 'personnel ships' – the Southern's *Biarritz* was one of them – were involved in these movements, which were successful in delaying the advance of the German Panzers from the southern direction. But a simultaneous drive by the enemy from the north left only Dunkirk as a possible point of exit. By the 29th the Southern was ordered by the Admiralty to make available *all* its ships grossing more than 1,000 tons and 150 miles range. On paper, this would have excluded such invaluable vessels as the 1920s-built cargo ships, of which two, *Hythe* and *Whitstable,* were to be so prominent at Dunkirk, even though their gross displacement was only 685 tons. Similarly *Tonbridge* would later be busy evacuating the Channel Islands, its cattle stalls filled with children, as we shall see. Meanwhile two SR vessels, the *Maid of Kent* and the *Brighton* had been bombed and lost at Dieppe on 23rd May.

By 25th May, it was possible to take off non-combatants, wounded and those not directly involved in holding up the enemy, using Dunkirk harbour, and here the Official History specifies that cross-Channel steamers were used. These included the SR's *Canterbury,* making the first of at least four emergency shuttle trips, in which she took off literally thousands of troops. Other railway vessels operating as hospital ships – the *Isle of Thanet, Worthing* and *St. David* – took on board wounded while under continuous air attack, while the company's *Isle of Guernsey,* exceeded her capacity for 'cot cases' by 50% on one journey. The Great Western's *St. Helier* was attacked by no fewer than nine

planes on this date; so much so that her master gallantly kept her at the Dunkirk quayside – rather than risk sinking in the harbour approaches. Mercifully, she survived, and the French coast was to see her many times subsequently in the next three weeks.

Preparations for a mass evacuation were not helped by an eleventh-hour decision to throw a fresh Canadian division into the battle, creating loading problems at a number of English ports, and potential disembarking problems on the other side. Fortunately, this order was countermanded, although not before the troops were embarked in their transport vessels, and promptly had to be turned out of them. Another unexpected problem which cropped up at Dunkirk on this date concerned water – there was a shortage of drinking water in the port, and consignments had now to be conveyed on a daily basis, both in tank loads and individual canisters. *Maid of Orleans* made one crossing with 600 water cans – and then had to make it all over again, unable to berth because of the intensity of the air attacks. She eventually loaded troops, along with *Canterbury* and *Rouen,* the last-named taking wounded to Cherbourg.

The 26th May was the official start of Operation Dynamo, at 6.57pm, although the commander, Admiral Ramsay, based at Dover Castle, had ordered evacuations to begin earlier that afternoon in view of the worsening situation. At 10.30pm that night, the first fighting troops returned to the UK.

Maid of Kent, *a Southern Railway ferry which entered service in 1925, was, like her Isle sisters, requisitioned as a hospital ship. Her red crosses failed to save her from the attentions of the Luftwaffe, however, and she was sunk at Dieppe in May 1940, before the Dunkirk emergency, in which all her company's ships were required to participate.*

The Great Western's St. David *was another hospital ship whose red crosses seem to excite the attention of the enemy. She survived the bombing and shelling at Dunkirk, but was badly damaged by a mine at Dover. Later* St. David *served in the Mediterranean, falling victim to the Luftwaffe when carrying wounded from the Anzio beachhead in January 1944.*

71

The Southern's Maid of Orleans *had a distinguished war record, serving in the infernos at both Dunkirk in 1940 and Normandy four years later. Only an accidental collision curtailed her service in evacuating the army in the first of these operations and it was a torpedo which terminated her career altogether in the second. It was some time before the agent of her fate was known; both the company's historian and the Official History published by the Admiralty described this illustrious vessel as having been mined.*

One problem which had been overlooked when railway and other passenger steamers were ordered on rescue missions to Dunkirk was the lack of charts. Obviously, cross-Channel ferries, whether plying the Irish Sea or the English Channel, would normally operate as shuttles between two ports, with little variation in their routes. This deficiency was to affect both hospital ships and what the Navy called personnel carriers, and was worsened by the fact that the presence of mines, sandbars and wrecked vessels reduced approach options to the beleaguered port of Dunkirk. The safest was probably Route Y, the longest and most northerly approach, which was 87 sea miles in length from Dover, proceeding north of the Kwinte Buoy and braving the shallows through the Zuydecoote Pass, although this could expose vessels to attack from E-Boats or U-Boats to the north. The middle way, Route X, was 55 miles but meant crossing the Ruytingen Pass, which was not advised for larger vessels, while Route Z, the shortest at only 39 miles, exposed ships to the Calais batteries.

The lack of navigational charts was to prove a recurring problem for civilian, or recently-requisitioned, ship captains at Dunkirk. This may have accounted for the Bristol Channel paddler *Brighton Belle* which struck a wreck on the 27th while ferrying 800 troops homewards. The fact that she was being attacked from the air at the time could hardly have helped, but fortunately, all complement and crew were taken off safely by another paddle steamer, the *Medway Queen.* The *Brighton Belle* had been built for railway service in the first year of the century as the *Lady Evelyn,* plying the Lancashire coast resorts for the Furness Railway.

On 26th May the Southern's *Isle of Guernsey* had to approach the Continental coast via Route X, playing follow-my-leader after the *Worthing,* as the latter was one of few vessels carrying relevant charts. There was a grim irony in the hospital ships' approach. Despite their Red Cross markings and the good visibility, the ships came under fire from enemy artillery at Gravelines, although the medical staff on the *Isle* assumed this to be practice fire from French batteries and carried on with their afternoon tea, taken against a background of gramophone music! They took off some 350 wounded on this occasion, continuing to make daily runs, the last coming on the 30th, when she loaded four

times as many wounded as she was intended to carry. Her master said later that "we made such a wonderful target for the aircraft hovering overhead with the flames of the burning port showing all our white paintwork up."

The *Isle of Guernsey* promptly ran aground while attempting to return on the 30th, only managing to escape after 45 minutes of exposure to any enemy plane looking for easy prey. Even then her adventures were not over, the Dumbarton-built vessel having to be guided out of a minefield by a Dover pilot boat. Again, the lack of navigational charts was almost as mortal as the lack of protection from air attack. On her last visit, the master of the former railway ship *Manxman* was so

angry at the casual way naval officers had treated him and his crew, leaving a hawser fouling his planned harbour berth, that he sailed straight out to sea from Dunkirk, avoiding any of the recommended channels, and reached home safe but angry.

By the 28th of the month, the harbour appeared to be targeted too intensively for continued use, with refineries at the western end on fire. It was decided to use three beaches east of the town – Malo, Bray and La Panne – the last of these, the farthest, stretching into Belgium. The first two ships which lay off the beaches soon found that bringing troops off in small boats was going to be impossibly time-consuming; if this was the only solution to embarking the BEF then the bulk of it was bound for captivity or worse. Two railway steamers, the *Paris* and the *Prague,* as well as the former Midland vessel *Manxman,* all had to endure air attacks while waiting stoically for troops to transfer slowly from the beaches. All three ships had already run aground in the Zuydecoote Pass owing to their masters' ignorance of local shoals and the Navy had belatedly given the *Prague* a set of charts. Fortunately, the naval officer in charge of the evacuation decided to experiment with calling larger ships to dock at the 1,400-yard eastern mole at Dunkirk harbour, despite its narrowness – only the width of three men – and the lack of mooring bollards.

Attempting to reach this improvised embarkation quay overnight on 28th/29th May was an LMS/LNER combination of the *Scotia* and the *Malines.* Approaching from the north, the steamers found destroyers engaging shore batteries, with Dunkirk itself under a pall of smoke. Indeed, so bad was visibility – this was not long after dawn – the ships overshot the port and were promptly shelled by enemy guns to the west of Dunkirk. *Scotia* took a hit in her engine room, but doubled back to the mole where she embarked no fewer than 3,000 British troops, some so exhausted they could hardly walk the length of the pier. Both of these noble vessels made it back to Blighty – and would return to France.

Later on that day the wind changed direction, unfortunately giving the Luftwaffe a clear view of operations at the pier. A furious assault followed in which the passenger steamers *Fenella* and *Crested Eagle* were set on fire and wrecked with great loss of life, as was a destroyer which was hurriedly pulled away from the harbour approach before sinking. The Southern's *Canterbury* was in the middle of this carnage, was hit and damaged, but struggled home with no fewer than 2,000 troops aboard. Around one-tenth of them were killed by bombing, along with 32 of her crew of 82, and she was out of action for nearly a week, but she would still go back. Her company sisters *Lorina* and *Normannia* now attempted to collect from the beaches, but with fatal results. Both were bombed and were sunk in shallow water, the *Lorina* losing eight of her crew of 49. Two days later, a mixed group of Guardsmen and destroyer crewmen were able to cut free the *Lorina's* lifeboats and put them to work in ferrying troops off the beach, so her loss was not totally in vain. Meanwhile, all of *Normannia's* 49 crewmen had been saved. Their ship settled on an even keel with all flags flying.

A bomber's eye-view of the Southern Railway's Canterbury. **This fine packet, built by Denny's of Dumbarton for the Dover–Calais passage in 1929, was long associated with the 'Golden Arrow' service before and after World War Two. During the war, she survived bombing while making a number of return journeys to rescue troops at Dunkirk, while for the D-Day landings she had her decks concreted over to facilitate landing troops and equipment. Returning to civilian life, she was the first cross-Channel ferry to be fitted with radar.**

Wednesday 29th May saw the paddle steamer-minesweepers come to the fore. Members of the 12th Flotilla – *Waverley, Marmion, Duchess of Fife* and *Oriole* – now approached, their comparatively shallow draft making them more suitable for embarking troops from the beaches than other ships of similar capacity. Hoping to maximise this advantage, on the morning of the 29th, the captain of HMS *Oriole* (previously *Eagle III* owned by the LMS) deliberately beached his craft literally within an arm's length of the troops waiting up their necks, and succeeded in passing some 3,000 of them the length of his deck to vessels behind. According to David Divine's account, this Clyde steamer waited until the evening of that day, frequently under fire, before succeeding in escaping with 700 soldiers and nurses on board. Of course, the grounding of one of His Majesty's ships was a matter of no small import and the commander involved, Lt. E. L. Davies, made a signal to the Admiralty reporting what he done – and said he would do this again, if necessary! (His action was in fact approved.)

What Mr. Divine does not mention is that the *Waverley* attempted to tow her fellow paddle-steamer off the beach even although her captain and crew were cleared to set sail for home. Having picked up 600 men from the beaches, the LNER steamer was ordered to form up on a cruiser offshore (probably HMS *Calcutta*) for protection from air attack, but asked for, and was granted, permission to try and pull clear the *Eagle III*. Her towing attempt failed, and under unrelenting attack from bombers, the *Waverley* set off homewards alone across the Channel. Tragically, her steering gear was put out of action, the Luftwaffe concentrated their fire on her, and she sank with more than 300 casualties.

One survivor was Captain John Cameron, acting as Navigation Officer on his own ship, and who deservedly was awarded the DSC. But that came later. In an interview with the BBC, Captain Cameron revealed that when he and his engineer later boarded an overnight train for Glasgow at Euston, two fellow passengers complained about such 'ragged' men being allowed in a first class carriage. When the guard learned the men's story, he refused to move the two shipwrecked sailors and told the complaining passengers to find seats elsewhere in the train. It was a tiny but heartening coda to a traumatic event.

Meanwhile, *Eagle III* returned to base – Harwich – safely, but turned round again within five hours. It took her some fourteen hours to return to Dunkirk, taking a Pathe newsreel cameraman whom, one crewman recorded, "had no idea what he was in for". Nevertheless, this grand LMS ship survived to make no fewer than five crossings, the last of them crewed by the men of HMS *Cambria* (in peacetime the Bristol-based Campbell steamer *Plinlimmon*). With her degaussing equipment faulty, it was decided not to risk the

Cambria, so she swapped crews with *Oriole* at Margate on 3rd June. Historian Russell Plummer recounts this interesting operation – not mentioned in either the Official History or by David Divine – and quotes an exhausted officer on the LMS steamer commenting on how much cleaner the Campbell vessel was when taken over in harbour. Sadly, the *Eagle III* would never paddle the Clyde again; although she survived the war, a new boiler and complete reconditioning was required, and was cancelled as uneconomic.

The Southern's cargo vessels built in the 1920s proved invaluable in World War Two, even if they officially were too small to be requisitioned for Dunkirk duty. One which served at Normandy in 1944 was Minster, *employed as a netlayer. Unfortunately, she struck a mine off the beaches, running aground with great loss of life. She could not be salvaged.*

The 30th May saw more drama involving railway ships. The North Channel ferry *Princess Maud* of the LMS set off for Dunkirk, perhaps unwisely, in daylight along Route Z. She was promptly shelled off Calais, being hit in two places including her engine-room. Four men later died of their wounds, but meanwhile water was pouring in through a hole three feet square. Refusing to succumb to this dire emergency, her crew plugged the damage with mattresses, while her master took countermeasures, including lowering boats on the opposite side as a counterbalance. Within five hours, she was back at Dover – empty – her crew bitterly disappointed that their fellow crewmen's supreme sacrifice appeared to have been in vain. But the *Princess Maud* was not finished yet, even if Lloyd's listed her as "reported to be sinking, but returned to base". She would go back to Dunkirk.

The LNER's *Prague,* normally to be found on the Harwich station, returned to Dunkirk three days after grounding on the Zuydecoote Pass and later having to wait for troops to be ferried out to her. It should perhaps have been obvious to the military mind that this vessel had too deep a draught (16 feet) for operations off such

One of the largest railway ships built between the wars was the LNER's Vienna, *seen here at Ardrossan in November 1943 in use as a depot ship for coastal forces. Intended for the Harwich–Hook of Holland station, she was requisitioned in June 1941, later being acquired permanently, and finally sold for scrapping in Belgium in 1960. Her two sisters* Amsterdam *and* Prague *were more spectacularly involved in wartime events, the former being lost off Normandy, the latter only narrowly surviving Dunkirk.*

---

a hazardous coast but her master and crew were determined to help, and on the 31st found troops to embark at what appeared to be a deeper part of the formerly closed harbour. Unfortunately this proved to be an illusion, and after embarking 100 tons of troops and equipment, found herself grounded again. Two tugs, combined with the *Prague's* own engines at full power, just managed to free her, with German shells bursting all around just to keep things interesting. She would return the following day.

Hospital ships continued their perilous task of collecting the wounded. The Southern's *Dinard* had already made two trips with stretcher cases from Cherbourg on the 25th and Dunkirk on the 29th, coming under air attack on the second of these mercy trips. On the 30th, her master took her alongside the Mole, despite the shallowness of the approach and the water turbulence caused by falling projectiles. Sailing in darkness on an ebb tide, the *Dinard* had to be navigated by torchlight, feeling her way, as it were, from buoy to buoy before reaching Blighty safely. She even had to throw her wheel over to avoid two torpedoes, as if bombs and shells were not enough hazard. This hardy Denny-built vessel was later damaged when supporting the D-Day landings and passed out of railway hands in 1958; she went on to complete no less than 50 years' service.

Another railway-owned hospital ship made waves of a different kind on the same day. Historian David Divine reports that the GWR's *St. David* declined to return to Dunkirk unless given a military escort. This was not forthcoming, although it should be pointed out that the ship had already made at least two journeys in harrowing conditions, her captain was medically certificated for exhaustion and her chief engineer was found wandering ashore suffering from loss of memory. But, after a period of rest and a change of captain, the ship would return to Dunkirk, on 31st May. On this latter occasion, there was no berth available and with heavy bombing continuing, the *St. David* withdrew. She

All the Great Western's 'Saint' class in World War Two saw war service, three of them as hospital ships. The St. Julien *was attacked at Dunkirk in 1940 despite displaying Red Cross markings but succeeded in taking off wounded. Later that year she tried to do the same at Brest, being bombed and machine-gunned as a result. She survived D-Day as well, despite being damaged twice.*

did not survive the war, being sunk while supporting the Anzio landings. On the same date, sister ship *St. Julien* reported that she had come under heavy shelling while loading at Dunkirk, despite her Red Cross insignia being perfectly visible in daylight. Although her master reported his crew as 'getting shaky', they assisted in carrying stretchers aboard and reached home safely.

Early on Friday 31st, the Southern's cargo steamers *Hythe* and *Whitstable* had been ordered to cross to Dunkirk, the former's master being disgusted with the 'army map' given him to navigate from! The vessels passed the sunken *Normannia,* her masts visible with flags flying, and then appear to have separated when they reached Dunkirk. The *Hythe's* master decided to take her alongside the Mole, despite enemy shelling. 674 men including wounded were embarked, the ship sailing after two hours under continuous attack. The crew passed the wrecked *Lorina* on their return trip, which was accomplished safely. Meanwhile, the *Whitstable* stayed offshore, having to relocate and anchor twice as the tide fell. For no less than six hours she awaited evacuees, with her master, Captain Baxter, understandably seething. "The method used for embarking the troops from the beach was that the soldiers rowed off in boats until they were in water deep enough for shallow draught launches to take them in tow... [these] towed the boats to the ships at anchor... we merchantmen were kept waiting in a very dangerous position while ships armed to the teeth came in, loaded up, and departed in an hour or so..."

Military historian David Divine, who recorded this criticism, suggests that the railway ship captain "was not in a position to see the whole picture". Perhaps not, but he was *in* the picture and the only instance of an unarmed, or lightly armed, vessel being afforded anti-aircraft protection appears to have been when the *Waverley* was offered a chance to shelter under the 'umbrella' of the anti-aircraft cruiser HMS *Calcutta*. But the *Waverley* was herself technically a warship and it does appear that the civilian ships simply had to run the gauntlet of enemy fire, with no assistance rendered unless they were sinking. Tragically, within a year HMS *Calcutta* herself was sunk – by enemy aircraft – when supporting the evacuation of Crete.

A ship missing from David Divine's account of Dynamo was the Great Western cargo vessel *Roebuck*. Successor to the Channel Islands steamer lost early in 1915, the second of the name was quietly unloading islands' produce at Weymouth when suddenly summoned to Dover. Her captain had assumed that she would not be used in the evacuation as his ship had not been 'degaussed', in other words demagnetised to ensure invulnerability against magnetic mines, but when ordered to proceed to Dunkirk he did not hesitate, setting off at two o'clock on the last morning of May 1940. Needless to say, he had no relevant charts. Off No.6 Buoy to the north of Dunkirk, the *Roebuck* was in collision with a fast-moving destroyer but fortunately both vessels were able to proceed, and the GWR ship took up a position off La Panne. Here, like other ships before and later, she found it impossible to embark any troops because of the offshore wind and was ordered to

the harbour instead. Despite being shelled, *Roebuck* took a berth on the western side, improvised necessary ramps, and loaded 570 troops and 99 wounded. Leaving at 3.35pm, she reached Dover safely four hours later but was unable to enter harbour until seven the next morning. After she had unloaded she was ordered back to Weymouth and would undergo demagnetising before undertaking more rescue work – of which there would be plenty. Magnetic mines were the least of rescuing ships' concerns at Dunkirk, but her captain and crew could hardly have known that and their courage was formidable.

The month closed with the loss of the Bristol-based paddler *Brighton Queen* which was returning on her second trip from Dunkirk with 600 troops when she was attacked from the air, the official records stating specifically that she came under gunfire. Her master was forced to abandon ship in an orderly manner, but while awaiting rescue it seems that some of the survivors were machine-gunned in the water. This vessel was formerly the *Lady Moyra*, built by the Furness Railway, now joining her sister *Lady Evelyn* at the bottom of the Channel while on national service.

Glorious June opened at Dunkirk under a canopy of smoke and continuing attacks from aircraft and artillery. June was less than ninety minutes old when the requisitioned paddle steamer *Whippingham* of the Southern Railway left the Mole with some 2,700 troops on what is believed to have been her only trip to Dunkirk. The Isle of Wight steamer gingerly made her way out of the beleaguered harbour in such an overloaded condition that her paddle-wheel housings were barely twelve inches above water level. She safely delivered her passengers – the equivalent of more than two battalions – and served her military masters for the rest of the war and the travelling public up to 1962. The *Whippingham* was not the only railway steamer busy on that Saturday, with no fewer than 64,429 men being lifted that day, despite no let-up in enemy attacks. Two destroyers were accounted for by the Luftwaffe outside the harbour before noon, with one rescuing tug also being sunk, some of her complement having to be rescued from the water twice in a single day.

Two railway steamers made their appearance on that summer morning. The LNER steamer *Prague* was back again, having already brought out over 3,000 men, but after taking on another 3,000, this time Frenchmen, she was seriously damaged in her engine room by dive-bombers. By judicious use of her remaining engine she got away from Dunkirk, but it was felt advisable to take off her troops, nearly all of whom transferred to three other vessels in mid-Channel – destroyer *Shikari,* corvette *Shearwater* and the (non-railway) paddler *Queen of Thanet* (which took no fewer than 2,000 troops off the Prague) – and all this at the steamer's best speed.

Towed by the Dover tug *Lady Brassey,* this gallant vessel limped back to Kent, before being beached near Deal. Both her master and chief engineer received honours for their rescue efforts. Nor was the *Prague* a total loss. She later became a hospital ship, making more than 50 journeys to and from Normandy after D-Day. Unfortunately, her return to railway service after the war proved temporary; she was mortally damaged in a dockyard fire in 1948.

While the LNER ship was limping home, the *Scotia* of the LMS moved in. Refusing to be intimidated by her previous experience, her crew had refuelled the ship – by hand, since she was a coal-burner and there were no mechanised loading facilities available – and she approached the enemy coast with a warning from a passing destroyer that it was "windy off No 6 buoy". This proved not be a weather prediction.

Arriving off No.6, the LMS ship was bombed, then bombed again after an RAF patrol had temporarily driven off the enemy aircraft. She was then near-missed as she approached the Mole on the west of the harbour where, perhaps surprisingly, her 26 feet draught did not prove to be a problem. She embarked some 2,000 French troops, and headed back towards No.6. Unfortunately she would sail no farther. No fewer than twelve aircraft attacked her in three relays of four, and the Denny-built vessel, whose predecessor had survived the Great War, was doomed. She rapidly took on a list and one bomb went down the rear funnel. Confusion reigned on the vessel, with the French troops unable to understand English commands and with three lifeboats smashed. When order was gradually restored, the destroyer HMS *Esk* came alongside or, more specifically, pressed her bow against the sinking ship allowing many men to transfer. Aircraft came over again, but the destroyer kept up an umbrella of fire. She then proceeded to the other side of the steamer and again took off as many soldiers and crew as it was possible to do. Nevertheless, some 200-300 Frenchmen were lost,

along with 30 of the railway ship's crew. As David Divine wrote, "The sinking of the *Scotia* was a tragedy ... but it might have been a very great disaster" had it not been for the coolness of two ships' captains, one naval and one civilian. Unfortunately, HMS *Esk* was also destined for a watery grave, striking a mine in the North Sea on 31st August that year and sinking with 160 casualties, including her gallant captain, Lt. Commander Couch.

Not surprisingly, the military would decide that daylight crossings were now too dangerous for ships whether RN or mercantile. In practice, there seems to have been little change in the largely improvised arrangements. Not only were British ships being targeted; the French Navy lost seven destroyers in as many days in assisting at Dunkirk. By 6.00pm on that first day of June no fewer than 100 bombers had vented their wrath on Dunkirk and its improvised shuttles. But this was to be the longest 24 hours of the evacuation and nightfall was still some time away.

One railway vessel had already crossed in daylight, and under tow. The Southern Railway's Isle of Wight vehicle ferry *Fishbourne* was thought to be too slow to be an asset at Dunkirk, but was taken across nevertheless. Here she endured air attacks without the compensation of having taken off troops, as her towing tug was assigned to other duties. The *Fishbourne* was then left to make her own way back to Ramsgate, empty. What the railway company must have thought of its vessel being effectively abandoned to make what would probably be a five-hour crossing unescorted in broad daylight is anyone's guess and the company history is silent on the point. Her sister *Wootton* stood by at Ramsgate for orders, but she was not asked to brave the Channel.

Meanwhile, other, faster ships did. On the day when Admiral Ramsay concluded that no more operations could be undertaken in daylight, the Southern's *Maid of Orleans* lay moored at the Mole at Dunkirk for no less than six hours. She facilitated the loading of two destroyers alongside her, before taking off 1,800 troops herself, reaching Dover safely. The Great Western's *St. Helier* was no less brave; arriving at Dunkirk during a bombing raid she remained at the Mole for some seven hours, with shells succeeding bombs, before leaving with a full load of troops. But still the civilian ships braved the enemy and came back for more.

Or would have done. Unfortunately, *Maid of Orleans* had made her last contribution to Operation Dynamo. Casting off again from Dover at 8.30pm she was

immediately in collision with a damaged destroyer, HMS *Worcester.* Invariably, when an armoured ship met a civilian one, it was the latter which came off worse, as happened here. The Southern's ship was too badly damaged to sail, although she would be repaired and would play her part at D-Day. David Divine records that she had been responsible for liberating 5,319 men from certain incarceration, adding "the utter disregard that this unarmed vessel showed for the almost intolerable dangers of the work and the limitless endurance of her people give her a high place in the record of famous ships."

Joining the Southern's Isle of Wight car ferries in 'standing by' for orders was a little vessel named *The Mew.* She was a GWR ferry which normally operated in the Dart estuary in Devon and was named after a prominent rock in the river there. Her railway crew took her along the South Coast into harm's way and, according to the company history, were eager to do what they could in helping with the evacuation. They must have had mixed feelings when they were ordered to return westwards. Although a slow moving vessel, she was surely no slower than the *Fishbourne* and could pack in 543 passengers as well as five vehicles, so she might have been a useful addition to the rescue fleet. In any event, the high mortality rate for the 30 knot destroyers proved that speed offered no immunity against bombing or shelling.

One of the saddest losses at Dunkirk was that of the Southern Railway's steamer Paris. *Originally built for the LBSCR, this attractive steamer made a number of trips to Dunkirk in 1940, successfully bringing off many troops and wounded, but succumbed to a Luftwaffe attack, with many crewmen killed. A stewardess had to be rescued from the sea twice after a lifeboat was machine-gunned.*

On the morning of 2nd June, the exasperated Captain Tennant, effectively commanding the evacuation from the French side of the Channel, sent a signal *en clair* to the local German commanders demanding immunity for hospital ships approaching in daylight for wounded only. Two hours later the *Worthing* of the Southern Railway weighed anchor and crossed the Channel. She was attacked by no fewer than twelve aircraft and, slightly damaged, managed to return safely, but without embarking wounded. Her messages were heard by another SR vessel-turned-hospital ship, the *Paris,* whose master, Captain Biles, queried whether he should proceed to Dunkirk in view of what had happened to his Southern colleagues. On being rather heartlessly told to do so, he unhesitatingly set off just before 5.00pm. The inevitable happened; the ship was attacked by no fewer

The Southern Railway's Isle of Thanet *made two trips to Dunkirk in 1940, surviving air attack, but was forced to turn back on two other occasions. She missed the end of the evacuation when she collided with and sank the Dover Examination vessel. In 1944 she landed troops at Juno beach in Normandy, surviving another collision before returning to SR duty in 1946.*

than seventeen aircraft, and had to be abandoned while under tow. Twenty of the crew lost their lives in this gallant gesture. One who was saved was a stewardess, a Mrs. Lee, although only after she had been machine-gunned in the water, rescued by a lifeboat and then blasted out of it again before enduring another 90 minutes in the sea. She was finally picked up by a passing tug and by the time her story was recounted in the company history, she was working in comparative safety as a carriage-cleaner at Brighton.

Despite these setbacks, more large personnel vessels prepared to cross on the 2nd. These included the GWR's *St. Helier,* the LNER's *Malines,* the Southern's *Autocarrier,* as well as the *Newhaven* and *Rouen* which were French-registered but part-owned by the SR. Incidentally, *Autocarrier* is recorded as having made a return crossing to Dunkirk before the end of May but,

because of some misunderstanding among local commanders, could not find a single soldier to embark. Now these vessels experienced mixed fortunes. The Great Western master was told that he and his crew had done enough already and would be spared another crossing. Captain Pitman refused the order to stand down, although he allowed the Navy to insert an officer-led party of ten to assist his tired crew. The *St. Helier* sailed that morning, following in the wake of *Autocarrier* and two other civilian ships. Three Isle of Man ferries attempted to join them, although two had to abandon the crossing, one being involved in a collision, while another failed to progress with an unfamiliar crew on board. All the railway ships survived this day. *Autocarrier* would return and one of the two French-registered vessels returned safely, although the *Rouen* stranded and underwent an agonising wait in Dunkirk harbour for the next high tide. The *St. Helier* meanwhile got away from France not long before midnight, damaged and taking water, but fully loaded and about to successfully deliver her passengers to freedom.

The *Malines* is recorded as having "left the [Dunkirk] area in the course of the afternoon without orders, and returned to Southampton". This was David Divine's description of what would, in a military force, be considered a serious court martial offence, but we have

already seen the pressure which civilian crews underwent off Dunkirk as "ships armed to the teeth came in, loaded up, and departed in an hour or so...", while unarmed passenger steamers were forced to brave bombing and bombardment while waiting for orders. It should be added that this LNER ship had already rescued some 1,500 troops and would be active later in June in three later evacuations from France and the Channel Islands. Historian Russell Plummer suggests that the management of civilian ships at Folkestone, whence *Malines* had come, and where two other ships had failed to emerge on this date, was not as enlightened as at Dover, where naval parties would be inserted into civilian ships to assist tiring or dispirited crews.

One of the recurring pressures facing servicemen in both world wars was the cyclic, *repetitive* nature of danger. No sooner was a scouting mission completed in No Man's Land in the first war, or a bombing raid accomplished over German cities in the second, when it had to be undertaken *again*. And this applied equally to the Dunkirk operation, where tiring ships' crews had no sooner braved bombs and shells to bring troops out than they were ordered to return, in some cases immediately, to the fray. Of course, 'fray' implies some kind of fight-back but in fact sailors on civilian vessels such as ferries and hospital ships had no means of fighting back. Each time they crossed could be their last voyage. With each trip, the pressure ratcheted up. No wonder there were instances of service being refused, of ships' crews declining to sail to France, or of leaving Dunkirk without being ordered to do so.

At 11.30pm on 2nd June, Captain Tennant notified his superiors back at Dover that "the BEF is evacuated". But still there were troops, mainly French, on shore, so the work went on. Within two hours, four more ships reached the Mole, but the French troops expected there had been ordered to dig defensive positions. Comparatively few were evacuated, and blockships were stationed ready for sinking to render the harbour unusable to the Germans. The *Rouen* still awaited the tide.

On 3rd June the sunrise was "hard and brilliant". Although there was now a strong easterly wind, the personnel ships accompanied the destroyers over for one last effort. The Southern Railway was well represented by *Autocarrier*, the indefatigable *Canterbury* and the French-registered *Côte d'Argent,* all loading French troops, the last-named more than a thousand of them. Meanwhile, the *Rouen* managed to free herself and apparently made yet another return journey to Dunkirk. She was a lucky ship with a brave crew during Operation

Dynamo; her luck ran out two months later when she was captured by German forces. Although she was later mined in the Baltic, she was able to return to her French operators after the war, but proved unsuitable for further passenger service.

Dynamo officially ended at 2.23pm on 4th June, with the last of the civilian vessels having left some twelve hours earlier. Many ships claimed to be the last to clear Dunkirk with troops, and authors appear to differ on this, but both historian David Divine and Poet Laureate John Masefield cited railway ships as among the last. Masefield singled out *Princess Maud* of the LMS for praise, rather curiously describing her as "that well known Channel steamer" – although she usually operated much farther north than the English Channel. She had arrived at Dunkirk, where she had experienced such a traumatic reception a few days previously, just before midnight on the 3rd. Entering the harbour, she took on troops, and "dogs of all description" as the company history recorded, but the crew were told that blockships would be sunk at 2.30am. The LMS ship got away with 40 minutes to spare, but while swinging clear "a shell fell in the berth we had just vacated", according to her master. Of *Princess Maud* and another late departure, the Medway steamer *Royal Sovereign,* David Divine said "with their departure, a great chapter in the history of the British Merchant Navy came to its magnificent close". Last of all appears to have been the destroyer HMS *Shikari.*

The Official History lists 848 ships, and vessels too small to be considered ships, involved in Operation Dynamo. Later authors, such as Russell Plummer, put the number at 1,300. The Official History credits destroyers with making the greatest contribution to the saving of the BEF; they "led the operation with selfless gallantry and suffered most heavily". While the bravery and skills of their commanders and crews was undisputed – and a number of them made three return trips a day – they at least enjoyed the protection of armour over and around them, capable of shielding them from all but a direct hit. In any event, Admiral Ramsay was ordered to release all but his oldest destroyers from Dunkirk duty on the 29th as their losses were unacceptably high. This was the day when the Harwich paddle steamers joined the fray.

But Royal Naval crews were part of a highly-trained, disciplined service; there was no question of them being reluctant to enter the war zone around Dunkirk and risk death and destruction. For civilian crews in unarmed vessels it was a very different matter. In contrast to the RN vessels, a railway ferry or other civilian vessel was comparatively 'thin-skinned' and could be sunk or disabled by even a near miss from a bomb, as befell the *Devonia,* not a railway steamer, but an innocent Bristol paddler which had hitherto spent her war exploring the Forth and the Farnes. She had never fired a shot or swept a mine in anger, but was disabled off Dunkirk – by a bomb which missed – on 31st May, and had to be beached and abandoned there. Equally, a collision with an armoured ship might very nearly account for a civilian vessel, such as the *Roebuck* or the *Maid of Orleans,* never mind whatever the Germans could throw at them.

If there are records of the crews of a (small) number of ships' crews refusing to return into what Priestley described as 'Hell', this underlines the courage they showed on earlier occasions, and which so many of their colleagues showed throughout. A hospital ship or cross-Channel ferry was big enough to provide a tempting target for artillery or bombers, without enjoying the armoured plating of even a minor warship. In his history, Captain Roskill does acknowledge their sacrifices, writing that "second only to the destroyers in the numbers of troops lifted came the personnel vessels, and they too suffered heavily".

Roskill relates that eight of these 45 'personnel' vessels were lost and nine damaged. He counted 230 fishing boats, as well as 38 minesweepers described as 'large' and clearly not converted paddle steamers. More than 200 privately-owned motor boats were involved and nineteen lifeboats. Later writers such as Mr. Plummer have produced even more comprehensive figures. A glance at Lloyd's lists, with page after page showing boats missing and sunk at Dunkirk, underlines the unhappy fact that no boat was too small to be considered a target from the Luftwaffe or from shore fire. (For a list of railway ships participating at Dunkirk, see Table V.)

Another of the GWR's 'Saints' was the St. Patrick, *whose military service appears to have been a solitary trooping voyage in 1939. She then continued the Fishguard–Rosslare service across the Irish Sea, succumbing to a Luftwaffe attack in May 1941 with much loss of life. Why she was unescorted on a route previously targeted by the Germans is unclear.*

As might be expected, Britain's railways also played a more conventional role in the Dunkirk story, in addition to the massive contribution made by their ships. No fewer than 575 trains were required to clear the returning troops from the ports, 325 of them from Dover alone, and with an average complement of 546 in each train. This does not include 31 specials out of Southampton and Weymouth, described by one of the companies' documents as 'not directly resulting from the evacuation'. (These may have been returning demolition parties or Guards' units previously sent across specially for perimeter defence.)

All trains proceeded to one of four 'Control Centres' – Redhill, Reading, Banbury and Salisbury – whence their destination would be assigned. Or, as more than one company history puts it "so the drivers could be told where to go". Curiously, French troops brought ashore were transported to Plymouth in order to return them to France. Although the burden fell principally on the Southern Railway, the Great Western had to find 142 locomotives for its share of the Dunkirk workings on 31st May and 1st June, while also handling 31 special trains, along with the SR and LNER, in response to a new programme of children's evacuations. The military histories give a passing mention to the Southern, crediting it with clearing the port areas of troops as quickly as possible, but the staff of all the railway companies really deserved enormous praise for their improvised organisation on the landward side of Operation Dynamo, as well as their courage in the face of the enemy at his most triumphant on the other side of the Channel.

With the Dunkirk evacuation having exceeded all expectations, the Admiralty did not hesitate to repeat it. In early June 1940, it was decided to attempt further troop embarkations from ports farther south on the French coast. In the case of Le Havre, this operation cost two LNER ships, and success was no more than patchy at other locations.

The Le Havre operation – codenamed 'Cycle' – began with a demolition party being ferried across to the port by the end of May. By 7th June, with the enemy closing, a force of nine Allied destroyers led a rescue fleet across, complete with Dutch powered barges, known as *shuyts* – these had also participated at Dunkirk – and with proper embarkation organisation onshore. This inevitably attracted air attacks and the Official History records the loss of the *Bruges* during this phase of Operation Cycle. This was a former Great Eastern turbine-driven steamer, built after World War One for the Harwich–Antwerp service. She had to be beached in a sinking condition, but fortunately all of her 72 crew were saved, and returned home on the *Vienna,* an LNER sister ship. Furthermore, some 11,000 British troops were taken off this hostile coast in what the Official History described as "a successful withdrawal".

It does not mention the loss of the unlovely *Train Ferry No.2,* which had to be beached and abandoned during Operation Cycle. She was listed by Lloyd's among civilian ship losses, with fourteen of her crew of 37 killed in this gallant act of attempted rescue. Returning unscathed was the Southern's *Worthing,* now a hospital ship, which had loaded wounded from lighters, and continued her run of good luck which had seen her safely through Operation Dynamo. Other ships had mixed fortunes in later evacuations.

The Great Western's cargo vessels *Roebuck* and *Sambur* were ordered to the nearby port of St. Valery on 12th June, but were unable to locate the naval vessel which would rendezvous with them before approaching the shore in the early hours of the 13th. The crew of a French fishing vessel told the GWR masters that it was safe to approach, which they did cautiously, noting "an LNER train ferry anchored close inshore" as they later reported (St. Valery was just east of Le Havre). The steamers were within one and a half miles of the shore when the coastal batteries opened up.

Hastily putting their helms over, the ships retreated, with *Roebuck* sustaining three fatalities. They were undoubtedly victims of poor communications. More than a week earlier, another Great Western vessel, the *St. Helier,* tried to approach St. Valery in darkness, failing to meet a promised naval escort, only to encounter a small boat showing lights and full of cheering, shouting men. They urged the ship towards shore, but the master's suspicions were justifiably aroused and he withdrew to home waters. Nevertheless, 13,000 Allied troops were picked up here, one of the railway steamers present being the *Duke of York* of the LMS. These ships came under fire, with at one stage the *Duke's* Chief Officer picking up a live shell from the deck and throwing it overboard, an action for which he was later decorated. But fog prevented a Dunkirk-style evacuation of the exhausted 51st Highland Division here, fated to be prisoners for the next five years, despite a fleet of nearly 200 small, mainly civilian, vessels waiting offshore on the 11th – "the only instance during this campaign", records Captain Roskill, "where a considerable body of British troops fell back to the sea but could not be rescued."

Rescue missions continued farther south on the French coastline, one of which resulted in the sinking of the liner *Lancastria* with horrendous loss of life, the worst to occur in all of the evacuations from France, and so bad that Churchill ordered news of it to be withheld for some time. Even later than this, on the 17th the *St. Helier* crossed to St. Malo and succeeded in taking off no fewer than 2,545 British and French troops, despite the local pilot advising against any approach to the port and refusing to assist. Three days later, this gallant GWR ship attempted an evacuation at La Pallice but was bombed and had to return empty-handed but safe. Meanwhile, on the 18th, her equally courageous Great Western sister *St. Julien* attempted to take off British wounded from Brest, which was rapidly becoming a major naval base for the *Kriegsmarine,* but the GWR vessel had to retreat while being bombed and machine-gunned. Not surprisingly, the railway company published a book by Ashley Brown recording the valorous feats of their ship crews, at Dunkirk and farther south (see Bibliography).

Later in June 1940, it was decided that the Channel Islands could not be defended so close to the Nazi-dominated Continent and by the 23rd of the month almost all the islanders who wished to leave had been evacuated by an armada of ships great and small. Some 17,000 residents were taken off Guernsey, 8,000 from Jersey and 1,500 from Alderney, the Southern Railway history recording the ultimate reception areas for them as being Bolton, Rochdale and St. Helens, for reasons not immediately obvious. As might be expected, SR and GWR steamers were involved in the evacuation, including the former's *Autocarrier* and *Tonbridge* and the latter's *St. Helier*. Less predictably, LNER ships also featured, including the *Archangel* which had stood by at Dunkirk and had taken part at St. Valery. (She was previously named *St. Petersburg* and we last met her ferrying the British and German ambassadors in opposite directions across the North Sea in August 1914.) Fellow LNER steamers also involved were the *Malines, Antwerp, Felixstowe* and *Sheringham* as part of an evacuation operation which, mercifully, was unattended by the Luftwaffe.

While the Official History gives the impression of a problem-free operation, it was far from being that. The Southern's *Tonbridge* was held outside Weymouth for no less than 30 hours awaiting entry to the harbour with island evacuees and, with only one nurse on board, there was much distress among mothers and children. Food was taken out to the ship – which was not a passenger vessel – and the children made as comfortable as possible for the night, sleeping in cattle stalls. One child, already ill, died in the evacuation overall and one was born. Parents who sent their children to England were denied news of them by the Nazi invaders until March 1941, when the Red Cross was allowed to deliver impersonal pre-printed notifications.

Just before German forces moved on to the islands on 1st July, the Southern Railway decided to make an additional evacuation from Guernsey and Jersey as late as the 28th of June, with their mailboat *Isle of Sark* braving what were now enemy waters. The reasons for such bravado are not immediately clear in the company history *War on the Line,* but some 250 passengers were taken to the islands and 647 evacuees safely brought back to Southampton. Not without incident; the Luftwaffe located the ship at Jersey before she proceeded on to Guernsey, and mounted a raid as she arrived there, believed to have killed as many as 44

people onshore. The last to leave was the Southern's own ticket-checker, a Mr. Prince, who, after completing his work at the Guernsey port, stepped on board the departing mailboat without first returning to his island home and with no luggage or personal effects. Two more island 'expeditions' planned by the Southern were now cancelled. No friendly vessel would return for the next five years.

Railway ships fought the second war against a backdrop different, and less varied, than in the first conflict. With Europe sealed off for at least three years, and the Mediterranean a 'no go' area even for the most hardened warships at one stage, it would seem that Britain's inshore shipping would have to remain as no more than that – part of the island's transport system duplicating the railways. While this was largely correct, in fact a number of railway ships took to the North Atlantic passage, either for cargo transport or for escorting, despite tonnage displacements which appear miniscule by the standards of today's merchant vessels and having to face hazards which today's crews would never have to worry about.

Among the vessels involved were four former Great Central (by then LNER) vessels intended for North Sea passages – the *Accrington, Bury, Dewsbury* and *Stockport,* but which found themselves roaming much farther and wider in World War Two. (Also included was the *Melrose Abbey,* described by the LNER history as belonging to an associated concern, in fact the Hull & Netherlands Company). None of the five appears to have interested the Navy in the first year of war, and coastal sailings, and even coal carrying, appeared to be the lot of the 30-year-old ex-GCR ships. But in 1941 it was decided to use all five of these Hull-built veterans as Atlantic convoy rescue ships, complete with hospital facilities and extra liferafts. The original idea was that they would accompany convoys only part of the way from the Clyde, but inevitably their range increased, even

The Southern Railway's ferry Isle of Sark *was the last civilian vessel to visit the Channel Islands before the Germans began five long years of occupation. She is seen here in 'uniform' while requisitioned in 1941-6. For most of that time she was used as a radar training vessel, but she returned to her peacetime run after the war, carrying up to 1,400 passengers at a time.*

Atlantic. On a more positive note, at least the *Bury* survived the war sailing the ocean, in contrast to her wretched experience of the previous conflict, tied up to a German waterfront for the entire duration. The company history records that this vessel picked up survivors from no fewer than four sinking ships within a 24-hour period.

as far as Newfoundland, according to the LNER's company history.

As rescue vessels, their presence was constantly required in all weathers. "That they survived at all", records maritime author Ambrose Greenway, "is a tribute to the strength of their original construction." One of the five in fact did not, the *Stockport* being torpedoed by submarine while taking rescued seamen to Iceland on 24th February 1943. At the time Lloyd's could only list her as 'presumed lost' and the company history published in 1947 still listed her as 'missing', although Mr. Greenway names U604 as her nemesis. Obviously, no survivors were rescued from the cruel

Mussolini claimed the Mediterranean as 'Mare Nostrum' and for some two years that was not an unrealistic description, with the Italian Air Force, hugely aided by the Luftwaffe from January 1941, able to impose air superiority in what was effectively an inland sea. More British capital ships perished or were disabled in the Mediterranean in that year than in all the other marine theatres combined. Fighting in North Africa took on a 'tidal' nature, with first one side advancing, then the other. But there was always the prospect of victory in the Middle East and southern Europe after Germany's

When newly established, the Southern Railway ordered a class of cargo vessels, all of which proved highly useful in World War Two, even if they did not emerge unscathed. One ship which survived was the Hythe, her most heroic moment coming when she took off troops from Dunkirk when the harbour was thought unusable. She was later recalled from a trip to the Channel Islands when the German occupation there was confirmed.

attack on the Soviet Union forced her to gradually cut back on her support for an ally who represented, in Churchill's phrase, a 'soft underbelly'. Following the Casablanca conference among the Allied leaders, it was decided to attack the European Axis through the Mediterranean. Civilian ships now suddenly were in great demand; major convoys were run to Malta and to Egypt, and the landings planned for North Africa, Sicily and then the Italian mainland itself would require troop carriers and logistical support. Surprisingly, despite the distances involved, railway ships had a part to play, and it proved to be a fatal one for a number of vessels, as described later.

Between Dunkirk and D-Day, Britain's railway ships settled down to a variety of tasks. Just as there was less emphasis on using paddle steamers for minesweeping for the technical reasons already given, there was also less need for such categories as 'auxiliary patrols' and 'armed boarding cruisers', while 'seaplane carriers', although in use at the outset of the war, were rapidly superseded by conventional aircraft carriers, and particularly the lighter escort carriers. Some Irish Sea ferries carried on as usual, although not without casualties.

One such was the *St. Patrick,* sunk by aircraft bombing when travelling between Rosslare and Fishguard on 13th June 1941 on the usual, if reduced, GWR service. She is described by Messrs. Duckworth and Langmuir as "probably the handsomest ship built for the Great Western", although technically her owners were the Fishguard & Rosslare Railways and Harbour Company, one which was not nationalised at the same time as its parent, the GWR, on 1st January 1948, no doubt because of its connection with independent Ireland, where it owned broad gauge mileage. The vessel had survived two previous attacks from the air, in the second of which she was strafed and a crewman killed, but the incident on 13th June was terminal. While attack on the western flank, while the *Duke of Wellington* of the LMS (formerly *Duke of York,* but now renamed in case of confusion, however unlikely, with the new battleship of that name) would carry reinforcements

for the eastern. In addition to carrying 250 troops, the latter had been adapted to carry ten assault landing craft on deck. (The *Invicta* carried six such craft and was soon damaged.) Tank landings were to take place in the middle area, on the beaches themselves, but in the event all 30 tanks used were lost. The fact that Mass Observers recorded public jubilation on hearing of the Dieppe Raid illustrates the misleading nature of official wartime propaganda, and not for the first or last time. At least, both railway ships survived this debacle.

Even a casual glance at Table VII will make obvious the fact that the greatest single source of danger for merchant ships plying inshore waters was enemy aircraft. Clearly, this was an unprecedented development; while there had been occasions when ships came under air attack in World War One, the weight of ordnance dropped on them was almost infinitesimal, as we have seen when British aircraft tried to bomb the German/Turkish battlecruiser *Goeben* in the Dardanelles in 1918. (Not only did she survive the attacks, she made it through the next war as well!) But 1939-45 saw a quantum shift in the development of aerial warfare and merchant ships were among the principal prey of new monoplane aircraft, complete with multiple machine-guns firing in the direction of travel, and mechanised bombing equipment. This change was particularly noticeable in the North Sea theatre. In the previous conflict, this was something of a 'mare nostrum' for the U-Boat until the mine barrages were put in place; previously there had been a steady and continuous predation of railway ferries and cargo vessels from the English Channel in the south to as far north as Shetland.

Enemy aircraft took over this mantle from the submarine and extended it to cover waters off the west coast as well. The German takeover of airfields in France and the Low Countries meant a potential for air attack even worse than British pre-war planners could have envisaged. While victory in the Battle of Britain in 1940 prevented an invasion, nevertheless, Britain was highly vulnerable to the German 'air weapon', particularly night bombing. We have already seen that

More closely associated with the 'Golden Arrow' service, the Southern Railway's Canterbury *had a busy war. She was involved in moving units across the Continent from the start and survived enemy bombing at Dunkirk. Later she was converted to troop carrying for D-Day, with the company history describing her decks as being covered with "some substance in the nature of concrete". Happily, she was to survive to resume the 'Golden Arrow' service after the war.*

---

paddle-steamers were being used as anti-aircraft 'batteries' in the Thames Estuary and these were supplemented in 1942, perhaps a little late in the day, by seven forts hastily assembled rather in the manner of present-day offshore oil installations, although on a smaller scale. Known as Maunsell Forts, they were equipped with searchlights and radar, as well as bristling with guns. Significantly, two of these, named 'Roughs Fort' and 'Sunk Head Fort', were manned by the Royal Navy off Harwich. Clearly, the port was regarded by the authorities as a major target for the enemy, but that was not how local people saw it. The LNER company

history stated that Parkeston Quay was "so rarely bombed, that the rumour spread that the enemy was keeping it intact for his own use". The crews of two former railway steamers might have been surprised to hear this theory.

This Essex port had seen increased Continental traffic in World War One, but by the summer of 1940, its ferries had nowhere to ply to. The Navy took over the Parkeston Quay complex in July, but had already established the 12th Minesweeper Flotilla here at the outbreak of war, four of its five vessels breaking off their work to travel to the Dunkirk beaches the following May, with three of the four returning. Harwich was well within the Luftwaffe's range, and two Scottish paddle-steamers were lost here. On 21st August 1940, the LMS-owned *Kylemore,* which had proved too slow to recommence her World War One career in minesweeping, was sunk by bombs off Harwich when working as a netlayer. On the following 9th April, in 1941, the LNER's *Marmion* was sunk in harbour, again by aircraft. It was found possible to raise her – her funnel had remained clear above water, proudly (and it has to be said, surprisingly), displaying her company colours – but the 35-year old vessel had to be written off as a 'constructive total loss'. More than 700 troops had been glad to embark on her at Dunkirk.

In contrast to the previous war, the only railway vessels lost to torpedoes in the North Sea in World War Two were sunk by E-Boats, a deadly development of the World War One torpedo boat, but with greater endurance. 'E' stood for enemy, but the Germans called these fast attack craft *Schnelleboote* or S-Boats. Around 115 feet in length, they were armed with up to four torpedoes and comparatively light armament, but their main threat was their speed – they were capable of 42 knots for up to 30 minutes. They used their pace to deadly effect, especially in night attacks, as they were otherwise vulnerable to RAF aircraft themselves. One part of the the English Channel was known as 'E-Boat Alley', and it was in the Channel, off Newhaven that they found their first railway ship victim. As already mentioned, this was the LMS (former LYR) freighter *Ouse,* which collided with another convoyed ship when avoiding torpedoes from an E-Boat on 8th August 1940. Coincidentally, their second railway victim was a 'Lanky' stable-mate, the *Rye,* torpedoed off Cromer in the following year, on 7th March 1941. No fewer than approaching Fishguard, the *St. Patrick* was struck by four bombs and sank within a few minutes, taking 23 of her complement with her, while 66 were saved. Looking back, it seems baffling that civilian vessels were not given some kind of escort protection when there was a record of enemy attacks on the route. A replacement vessel was commissioned in 1947 and immediately became part of British Railways. Another ferry which fell to the enemy was the *Portsdown* and her loss is described in the section on mine development.

Freight shipping was undertaken around the British Isles under escort, mainly to reduce the pressure on the railways. Ironically, it meant that the railways' own ships, which would normally have traded to and from the Continent, were now conveying bulk cargoes between north and south, effectively rivalling their owners' rail operations. That this could happen proved how far Governmental control of transport had progressed since 1914 when the then-new REC struggled to exert its influence on co-ordinating transport, whether by land or sea.

North Sea convoys were now running between the Thames and the Forth, comprising up to three dozen ships under way in either direction on six days a week. These voyages were particularly dangerous for both the merchant ships and their naval escorts, and not exclusively because of enemy action. Difficulties in ship handling were made worse by adverse weather conditions, particularly in winter, at night, or in poor visibility; railway historian Michael Joyce, who served in the North Sea theatre, told this author that his escorting destroyer HMS *Wallace* was in collision with other ships on no fewer than three occasions. (Incidentally, Mr. Joyce's section head on board was none other than Prince Philip, who often complained that nobody paid any attention to his orders – not the usual impression one has of HRH!)

The North Sea was not the only 'internal' shipping route and there was considerable traffic between the Bristol Channel and Plymouth, comprising some twenty ships sailing every two days. A convoy cycle was run between the Thames and Portsmouth every six days, involving eighteen ships, and on 8th August 1940 the LMS cargo vessel *Ouse* sank off the south coast in convoy, colliding with another vessel while attempting to evade torpedoes from a German E-boat. The *Ouse* had been built on Tyneside in 1911, and was one of the former Lancashire & Yorkshire vessels named after northern rivers. She had been briefly requisitioned to help evacuate St. Malo and was not the last former LYR vessel to succumb to E-Boats, as explained later.

Another shipping route introduced to reduce rail congestion was between the Northern Isles and Aberdeen. Scapa Flow in Orkney was the location of the main fleet base in World War Two as in the first conflict, even if the Home Fleet was a fraction of the size of its predecessor, and there was an associated RAF presence. Servicemen and supplies had to make their way tediously between the Pentland Firth ports and the south via the Far North line of the former Highland (then LMS) railway, all of it single track almost as far as Inverness. The author's father was stationed with the RAF in Orkney and could not believe how slow the trains were on the Highland line. Not surprisingly, there was an increase in offshore traffic between the islands and the ports farther south on Scotland's east coast. The enemy soon worked this out for themselves and accounted for the *Archangel* on 16th May 1941, bombed by the Luftwaffe a few miles off Aberdeenshire. Her crew managed to beach her, formerly the Great Eastern's *St. Petersburg,* which had ferried the enemy ambassadors in opposite directions on successive passages in August 1914, but the vessel now broke in four. For their gallant action no fewer than 40 of the 75 crew lost their lives, but only twelve out of 400 troops aboard were lost.

In August 1942 Mass Observers were reporting public acclamation on hearing of the triumphant Dieppe Raid. This was an amphibious landing intended as little more than a nuisance attack on the German-held French coast, but designed to satisfy public demand for action to relieve enemy pressure on the Soviet Union. Canadian forces were in the forefront, ferried to the French coast by a fleet of vessels including tank landing craft and the railway ships *Invicta* and *Duke of Wellington.* Volume 2 of the Official History, published in 1956, commented that "in retrospect it is plain that the plan suffered from several serious defects", but more recent research published by historian David Reynolds suggests that the participation of so many different services – the Navy, Royal Marines, RAF and Canadian Army – ensured that the planning was confused from the start, although any historian's view of the raid may be the result of so many military commanders covering their tracks afterwards. Whether well-planned or not, the element of surprise was lost when the attackers blundered into an enemy patrol and from that point onwards failure was a certainty.

For the fact was that the Dieppe Raid was a disaster, with great loss of life, and had no value except to convince those planning the much-awaited 'Second Front' that an opposed landing was not to be undertaken lightly. For the record, the Southern Railway's *Invicta* ferried men of the South Saskatchewan Regiment to 24 crewmen died. She was the second of her name to meet a violent end, the LYR losing its first *Rye,* built in 1914, torpedoed off Newhaven in April 1918. Four other merchantmen were torpedoed in this 1941 attack, with

an additional two going down off the East Anglian coast the next night. Meanwhile, U-Boats were seeking business in greater waters, becoming a constant spectre threatening vessels crossing the North Atlantic for the best part of four years. This was one battle in which railway vessels played a supporting role – specifically the four former Great Central freighters adapted as rescue ships from 1941. This is where the *Stockport* met her end and she was the only railway ship definitely known, by the end of the war, to have been torpedoed by a U-Boat.

Winston Churchill predicted early in the war that the magnetic mine would pose major problems, causing a rethink on how to deal with this insidious weapon – one which could now be dropped by aircraft into inshore waters where a submarine minelayer would be unable to penetrate. In practice, conventional contact devices were more of a problem initially and were tackled with gusto by sweeping flotillas almost entirely composed of paddle steamers. How they fared, and how they were gradually found different roles, has already been discussed. The effect of pressure and magnetic mines really came to the fore in the conquest of Normandy, where ships had to venture into coastal waters where defenders had had years to prepare for them, so railway steamers' encounters with more sophisticated mines will be left to the section of this book on D-Day and its aftermath.

We have already seen that the first mine victim was the *Mersey,* which succumbed to a magnetic device on St. George's Day 1940. Two other ships perished that year to more conventional mines, possibly their own. The *Princess Victoria* was mined in an area where she herself had been active as a minelayer and when a large vessel was sowing, say, a field of 270 mines (the capacity of the SR train ferries), it needed little in the way of a handling error, or a loose connection to a 'sinker' intended to anchor the mine underwater, to cause a catastrophe. Another LMS steamer, the Clyde paddler *Mercury,* is listed in the Admiralty list as "sank after damage by own mine, south of Ireland". She had been

A 1944 shot of the the north Clydeside port of Craigendoran. This was the base for most NBR and LNER operations on the Firth and the paddler nearest the camera was the Lucy Ashton*, the mainstay of LNER services on the Clyde in World War Two. Her record of service, including only two days when she failed to take up her station, was the subject of favourable comment among high-ranking company officials, as shown in archival files. Farther from the camera is the* Fair Maid*, an LMS vessel requisitioned for five years in World War Two and not returned to civilian life. The sleek lines of a destroyer can be seen in the right background.*

taken into tow, but could not be saved. In the following year, two Southern paddlers were lost, one on passenger service, one while minesweeping. The latter was the *Southsea*, severely damaged by an explosion off the Tyne on 16th February, when she became the casualty that was expected for every 80 mines swept. Although her crew succeeded in beaching the ten-year old vessel, sister to the *Whippingham*, she was declared a total loss.

The other mine casualty in 1941 was the *Portsdown*, and we have an eye-witness account of the sinking of this Dundee-built vessel on 20th September. One crewman, a Mr. Jupe, had heard a scraping noise on the port side just after the ferry had left Portsmouth, followed by "a terrific explosion. I had been looking out across the port bow and I was thrown into the sea. When I came to the surface... I swam to the after port side sponson, and assisted in getting out the lifeboats".

Despite his brave (and understated) endeavours, twelve passengers and eight of the crew of eleven perished, although a Naval pinnace was able to pick up seventeen passengers. Not only was this incident a tragedy for the Southern Railway, but the Royal Navy must have been horrified at the prospect of a mine so close to its principal base. The port and city of Portsmouth was of course a prime target for the Luftwaffe, and on a less serious note, there was one occasion when an unexploded bomb lodged in a building on the company's quayside. Southern Railway staff seemed quite prepared to work around it as normal – as long as the device was ticking! They ensured that the newspaper supply to the Isle of Wight from the quay was uninterrupted and no doubt made alternative transport arrangements when the bomb finally went off, which it certainly did, fortunately without casualties.

The loss of the Southern's steamer *St. Briac* – as sister of the better-known *Dinard,* was caused by a mine off Aberdeen on 12th March 1942, although whether it was conventional or 'influence' is not known. Thirteen of her crew were lost. While her sister was converted into a hospital carrier and served with distinction at both Dunkirk and off Normandy, the Clyde-built *St. Briac* was rather alarmingly designated as a 'Fleet Air Arm Target Vessel'. Messrs. Duckworth and Langmuir believed that she was present at Dunkirk, although this is not confirmed by other writers. The unfortunate *St. Briac* was the last railway ship to be mined in home waters.

In the Mediterranean theatre, railway ships found that the threat from the air was highly potent in an area where no part of the sea was far from an enemy airfield. On 19th February 1942 the Italian fleet still had sufficient capital ships to worry naval commanders, but it was aircraft which caused most ship casualties. The Official History describes efforts in that month – efforts made in vain at that time – to revictualise Malta, a number of merchant vessels being sunk. Among them on the 22nd of the month was the Turkish vessel *Hanne.* She was none other than the former *City of Bradford,* the one-time Great Central ship seized by the Germans at the outbreak of World War One. The otherwise authoritative history by Messrs. Duckworth and Langmuir stated that she was scrapped when sold by the LNER in 1935, but enemy bombs in fact claimed her. As if bombs were not danger enough, torpedoes could also be launched from the air and another LNER ship, the *Malines,* found this out in July 1942, torpedoed and beached off Alexandria. She was refloated and subsequently stationed as a training vessel in Egypt but would never carry passengers again.

One railway ship which served in the Mediterranean without mishap was the *Antwerp.* A sister to *Malines,* this former Great Eastern ferry was sent to Mediterranean to serve as a convoy escort vessel – the long way round, via the Cape of Good Hope – but in July 1943 she was chosen as Headquarters Ship for Operation Husky, the invasion of Sicily. From her, Admiral Ramsay, of Dunkirk fame, commanded the naval forces involved in a successful operation. The Official History was not above criticising this vessel however, commenting that she was "actually too small to serve as a HQ ship". She later became a radar picket ship, adding this role to her previous ones of evacuating the Channel Islands and escorting merchant ships, as well as (inadequately, it appears) providing a platform for a naval commander and later working as a leave ship for the newly-installed British Army of the Rhine immediately after the war. She was withdrawn in 1950, but without having resumed her civilian career.

A later invasion operation in Italian waters accounted for another railway ship. The Great Western's *St. David* was operating in the Mediterranean as a hospital ship and it was in this guise, and with her Red Crosses perfectly visible, that she was sunk by the Luftwaffe in the landings at Anzio on the Italian mainland on 24th January 1944. This was an amphibious assault undertaken south west of Rome and higher on the peninsula than the Allied armies had already reached, so an opposed landing was hardly unexpected. In the case of the GWR steamer, she was 25 miles out from Anzio, leaving the area when attacked. Casualties on board amounted to 57, including her master. Perhaps this setback might have been anticipated; the US Navy had lost four destroyers sunk or damaged here in the previous 24 hours. Hospital ships were now immediately dispensed with, landing craft being substituted to carry the wounded out of the beachhead area. The *St. David* was the last Great Western ship casualty, the ending of a record of loss which began at Scapa Flow 29 years previously.

The Normandy landings – the long-awaited Second Front code-named Operation Overlord – began in the early hours of D-Day, 6th June 1944. By mid-morning, Mass Observation diarists were recording that civilians back in the UK seemed to be fully aware that something momentous was happening, tuning in eagerly to the BBC news at lunchtime. The initial landings were a success, despite deteriorating weather and strong resistance encountered by the Americans on their allotted beaches. In particular, British shipping losses were much lighter than anticipated in the first fortnight after invasion, compared with US losses, although that was to change in the latter part of June.

As usual, military commanders appear to have held a robust view of how civilian ships could hold their own in the van of an opposed landing and this was evident on D-Day where there was no question of railway ships, for example, being kept safely in the rear. It was almost like Gallipoli, when Edwin Pratt had recorded that the railway steamers proved useful for "drawing enemy fire away from the battleships"! At least, this landing was carefully organised, but may very well have achieved the success it did as the enemy awaiting the Allied forces believed the weather to be too inclement for an attack on 6th June. Certainly, the weather was to prove a problem for ships military and civilian.

Railway ships were present from the earliest part of the assault, coming under fire and suffering some sea damage on the morning of the 6th, although the Official History unfortunately fails to mention them. It relates that the actual assault of the beaches, known as Operation Neptune, was undertaken by 1,213 naval ships and landing craft, and these included unarmoured civilian vessels. At Dieppe, the *Invicta* and *Duke of York* had ferried a total of sixteen small landing craft on their decks and while this 'piggy back' method of transporting troops was continued at Normandy, there

was also a veritable armada of barge-like vessels (LCs, LCTs, LSVs) mostly with ramps or bow doors, making their way independently across the Channel.

The railway ships, in the guise of troop carriers, HQ ships and hospital carriers, helped make up no fewer than 4,126 support vessels enumerated in the Official History. Of these, cross-Channel ferries were classed as LCI(H) – infantry carriers with davits operated by hand. On average, such ships carried up to 830 troops, roughly a battalion, with six to ten landing craft awaiting lowering. These LCAs would make more than one trip to the beach, in theory, and their transports included four Southern Railway cross-Channel ferries – *Biarritz, Canterbury, Isle of Guernsey* and *Maid of Orleans* – enlisted to carry troops to the beachheads, with the *Dinard* continuing as a hospital ship. The *Canterbury* was now unrecognisable as the vessel which had represented the marine element of the 'Golden Arrow' service in peacetime. Her four lounges were now stripped and hung with hammocks for troops, new davits fitted for assault craft, and her decks strengthened with what the SR company history cautiously described as "some substance in the nature of concrete". Happily, she was to survive to resume the 'Golden Arrow' service after the war and became the first Channel Packet to be fitted with radar.

Other Southern vessels acquitted themselves well. Two of the Isle of Wight paddle-steamers, their numbers reduced by the loss of the *Portsdown,* had come under military discipline in the build-up to D-Day, involved in practice runs carrying troops out to transports waiting in the Solent, and forbidden to contact shore while the exercises lasted. This tendering work began 'for real' for the *Merstone* and *Shanklin* from 3rd June, at a time when it was said (without too much exaggeration) that it was possible to walk from Portsmouth to Southampton by stepping from ship to ship. The invasion fleet included the *Isle of Guernsey,* no longer a hospital carrier but a

L.N.E.R. STEAMER "TALISMAN"

One of the first diesel-powered paddle boats in the world, the LNER's Talisman *rendered excellent service in World War Two as* HMS Aristocrat, *operating as an AA boat on the Thames. She later served as an HQ ship when the Mulberry harbour was being assembled at Normandy, during which service she was damaged by gunfire. She returned to civilian life with the LNER and later BR until 1967.*

troopship, and she made at least two trips in the first week of the invasion with 800 men on board on the second occasion. She survived the war.

But back to D-Day when the old reliable *Maid of Orleans* found conditions so difficult off Normandy that she was holed and slightly damaged by assault craft while disembarking troops. The steamer had anchored off the beaches at 5.40am and lowered all her own assault craft within 25 minutes. Powered landing craft came alongside – she carried more troops than could be accommodated in her own landing craft – but the sea was so rough that she had to be manouevred to provide lee shelter for these and five of her own craft returning,

so oil had to be poured to windward to try to calm the waves. The *Canterbury* was luckier, releasing her boats without difficulty, despite the rough sea. Her master, Captain Walker, felt particularly sorry for the troops as their craft made their shorewards, believing that even this short voyage would inevitably make them seasick. With everything having gone so well, he confessed later to feeling a certain sense of anti-climax. His colleague on the *Maid of Orleans* had no such luxury. When leaving the beachhead, his ship had to make smoke to evade enemy gunfire from shore batteries – although not the first time the *Maid* had experienced this!

Another member of the invading armada, although not until D-Day+1, was the Southern's *Biarritz* whose crew were reportedly indignant at missing the excitement of 6th June. They had all the excitement they needed on that next day, when a coastal battery located her at anchor off the French coast and, according to Bernard Darwin's book *War on the Line*, her master played the mouth organ to distract the crew while under fire! She was to make no fewer than fifteen trips to Normandy by the end of July, covering 9,000 miles. Needless to say, she was not mentioned in the Official History.

Before June was out, naval forces off Normandy found themselves opposed by an enemy they must have thought they had mastered – the mine. Four million of them had been sown off what the Germans called the 'Iron Coast', but Rommel, commanding forces in the sector, had asked for 100 million, an indication, if one were needed, of their reputation as defensive weapons. Of those in place, 'pressure' mines proved to be a major obstacle. These could not be swept conventionally, and would be triggered by a vessel working on full power, as a landing craft was likely to do approaching a beach. Once the danger was identified, all vessels had to proceed slowly in and out of the beachheads. Nine vessels, five of them warships, were lost in the second fortnight of the month but, as Table VII shows, this was nevertheless the most prolific ship killer the invasion fleet faced overall.

Some famous railway steamers, including a number which survived everything the enemy could throw at them at Dunkirk, were not to escape their encounter with mines off Normandy. The SR's *Minster* was accounted for in Seine Bay on D-Day+2. She was one of the nine freighters introduced by the Southern in 1924-8, within its first few years of existence, and, converted to netlaying, was one of three lost in the war; one of her sisters survived into the 1960s. Narrowly avoiding the same fate was the Southern's *Dinard,* mined as she approached Juno Beach to collect wounded some 24 hours after D-Day. Two minesweepers took off most of her complement, the remaining crew managing to keep her seaworthy, but it was decided to use a tug to tow her inshore where temporary repairs were made. Two days later she managed to limp across to Southampton, with her bow "nearly falling off", as the company history records, and she then entered dry dock. Six weeks later she was back in commission.

Another Southern vessel which fell victim to a mine was the illustrious *Maid of Orleans.* After her heroics at Dunkirk, this Dumbarton-built vessel was one of four Southern ships which had been involved in training exercises off the west coast of Scotland – so many of them that the crews were in danger of becoming 'stale'. The *Maid* had also been entrusted with ferrying the Prime Minister and senior military planners in acting as a tender for the *Queen Mary* at one time. When she met her end off Selsey Bill on 28th June, she was returning from delivering 800 troops to the beaches (according to the company history, although the Mulberry Harbour was in use for personnel by this time). Her usual

commander was not on board on this occasion, being replaced by Captain Masters, more frequently commanding the company's *Autocarrier.* Like his crew on the *Maid,* he had had little sleep for three nights. They now found themselves having to deal with a hull holed on the starboard side and a complete power failure. Four lifeboats and a landing craft were launched safely, with the gallant stand-in captain and four officers remaining to the last. Happily they were rescued, the *Maid* taking some 30 minutes to sink, with five men killed. She had been a grand ship and her name was perpetuated by a replacement vessel after the war.

The Admiralty classed her as a submarine's torpedoed victim in their 1947 listings and the U-Boat involved was later identified as U988, but the Southern's historian in 1946 believed a mine was to the agent of her destruction, and the Official History unusually named a civilian vessel, by mentioning the *Maid* (in a footnote, only) as having been mined. The loss of the company's cargo vessel *Fratton,* on 18th August, was also 'credited' to a submarine, although the company history is silent on her sinking when at anchor in Seine Bay.

Another railway ship bearing a famous name, which became a casualty off Normandy was the LNER's *Amsterdam,* which had survived the Orkney–Aberdeen passage which accounted for the *Archangel.* Successor to the Great Eastern steamer which was the last out of Antwerp after the German invasion in 1914, she carried United States Rangers to the Normandy beachhead and then sailed for the Clyde where she was refitted to carry casualties. A realistic development for an infantry carrier, unfortunately, although the *Amsterdam* was not to survive that role. (See Tables VI and VII). On 7th August 1944 she was one hour out, taking 400 wounded homewards, when there was an explosion. Although she sank in eleven minutes, the crew unselfishly assisted their charges into the boats, with the loss of up to 60 of them (casualty figures vary, but the low proportion of wounded who were drowned speaks volumes for the dedication of the crew). Among them was the ship's Matron who insisted on staying to the last and went down with the ship. All the engine room staff perished, a common occurrence on large ships where the only means of escape was by ladders easily buckled or loosened by explosion. As late as 1947 the Admiralty could only presume that the agent of this terrible loss was a mine.

gantry and in the aftermath of D-Day she was to prove indispensible.

By November 1944 the train ferries were operating once again into Calais and leave ships were running from there across to Dover by the following month. At home, there was a feeling that the war was over at last, the German counter-attack through the Ardennes coming as an unpleasant shock, its success possibly ruined only by a shortage of fuel for the Panzers. Following that temporary reversal, leave was organised on a major scale, some 90,000 British servicemen travelling in 1,881 trains away from Harwich and the two main Kentish ports in less than six months. The US Army used Southampton, but it still meant work for the Southern. Prisoners-of-war were guest patrons of the company's trains, 440 specials being laid on in six months to transport them to transit camps – Kempton Park on the Southern and handing over to the GWR for Moreton-in-the Marsh. As for the wounded, they were brought back from France as early as 7th June and we have already seen the cost to the crews of the ships

themselves, as in the case of the *Amsterdam* and the *Dinard*. Nevertheless, in June 1944 no fewer than 104 ambulance train workings had to be organised at ports on the south coast, each catering for 300 wounded. At least, there was an improved prospect of recovery for them; with the industrial production of penicillin, there was now an antibiotic which would deal with infected wounds and improve the prospect of returning injured men to health.

A sad end for a gallant LMS paddle steamer. HMS Oriole *was actually the Clyde vessel* Eagle III *and served heroically at Dunkirk where she was beached for some twelve hours on one of a number of mercy trips. In 1946 it was found to be uneconomic to recondition her, fulfilling the Admiralty's original warning in 1914 that rail companies might not want their ships back once the RN had finished with them.*

Another LMS ferry participating in the Normandy landings in 1944 was the Princess Margaret, *taken from the Stranraer–Larne service and converted into an infantry landing ship. In this guise she landed commandos at Sword Beach and made subsequent crossings with other troops before resuming her peacetime role.*

The last mine victim among railway vessels at war was a particularly sad one, at least to railway enthusiasts. On 17th March 1945, with only six weeks of the war still to come in Europe, LNER *Train Ferry No.3* was sunk off Dieppe. She had been blessed with the curiously twee name of HMS *Daffodil* and she became the second of this class of three World War One vessels to be lost, after *Train Ferry No.2* had been rashly exposed to the German guns at Le Havre in June 1940. Unfortunately, according to one report, she took a cargo of locomotives to the seabed. Casualty figures were not published.

The Southern's three train ferries survived the war and had found plenty of work once the Allies had established themselves in   Normandy by August 1944. Their use required a quay for loading and unloading as a minimum requirement, but the lack of cranes in French ports was anticipated and the ships had special lifting gear built on to their sterns. These contraptions were effectively a combination of derrick and crane, adding more than 250 tons to the displacement and jutting out 35 feet beyond the stern. These would lift a vehicle from a dock rail

section even if it were at right-angles, handling loads of 84 tons at a time. This would be adequate for its task; an 'Austerity' 2-8-0 designed by Robert Riddles for the War Department weighed in at 70 tons without tender, his 2-10-0 at 78 tons. A Stanier 8F 2-8-0, adopted earlier by the military and shipped overseas in large numbers, weighed 72 tons without tender. Locomotives were of course uncoupled from their tenders for transit purposes; railwayman author Charles Meacher recounted a story about a dockside crew in the Middle East who unloaded tenders the wrong way round!

Each SR ferry could carry sixteen locomotives if required, as well as whole trains. The *Twickenham Ferry* is recorded by the company history as having taken a hospital train of eighteen vehicles, fourteen of them carriages, to Cherbourg, where her lifting gear was certainly necessary in 1944 – the Germans had thoroughly sabotaged the pre-war port facilities, which American engineers literally built over with a steel-framed staging. US troops also featured prominently on board the *Hampton Ferry;* eighteen of them operated the lifting equipment, working amicably with the railway crew "like the most docile of demons", as the SR historian Bernard Darwin records. Incidentally, the records are unclear about Government use of the *Shepperton Ferry*. Pressed into use as a minelayer immediately after war was declared, she and *Hampton Ferry* were used on the Stranraer–Larne route (as road vehicle ferries) and it was during a repair at Belfast in May 1941 that HMS *Shepperton* was damaged in an air raid. She was modified three years later with a stern

While an examination of railway company archives reveals no irritation among officials about the loss – in some cases, permanently – of their vessels as the war went on, they had to consider what level of service their fleets could offer the public once victory was assured. In March 1944 the LNER's Scottish District Manager Tom Cameron (later head of BR's Scottish Region) made a strong case, writing to Chief General Manager Sir Charles Newton at company HQ (temporarily) based at Hitchin, for an entirely new vessel for the company's Clyde services. The *Waverley* (third of that name) had of course been lost at Dunkirk and it was clear that the compensation for her and sister ship *Marmion,* sunk at Harwich, was sufficient to build at least one brand-new replacement. Two vessels then expected to complete war service – the *Talisman* (HMS *Aristocrat*) and the *Jeanie Deans* – would require extensive overhauls on their return to railway service. Despite two losses, Cameron argued for only one replacement. From his description of immediately pre-war services from both his own company and the LMS, it was obvious that he expected the demand for Clyde sailing to continue a gradual but perceptible decline and the two companies had 'pooled' some services at off-peak times.

In the meantime, the 56-year-old *Lucy Ashton* was handling all the LNER's Clyde traffic single-handedly, all the year round. This former NBR vessel of some 270 tons displacement was not requisitioned in either war, but gave sterling service to her owners and the region's travellers and the diminished number of holidaymakers. Although designed for 'sheltered waters', she was daily

While a Caledonian paddler Duchess of Hamilton *succumbed to a mine in 1915, her LMS turbine-powered successor survived World War Two, operating on the Stranraer–Larne route. A particularly handsome vessel, she made her last revenue-earning voyage in 1969.*

---

exposed to passages which counted as open sea and in the years 1939-43 she clocked up 114,477 miles and carried 859,768 passengers, according to Cameron. All repairs had to be carried out at weekends – presumably out of season – apart from a two-day interregnum following a collision. "I think you will agree that this is a highly creditable performance to the ship and to our Marine Department" Cameron memoed Newton.

As we know, the Scottish manager was successful in his argument for replacement and hundreds of thousands of trippers, by no means confined to north of the Border, have now enjoyed coastal cruising on the *Waverley* (IV) – the result of this correspondence. Her existence says much for Cameron's powers of advocacy, for the LNER was not overactive in ordering replacement vessels post-war and certainly ordered no other paddle steamers.

The replacement steamer's first master was a certain John Cameron who nearly perished with the previous *Waverley* as she turned back to help a sister ship in trouble on the beaches of Dunkirk.

Chapter 8
POST-WAR

With the war over in 1945, all four of the major railway companies published accounts of how they, and their ships, had contributed to victory, although the editorial styles vary considerably. First to appear was *Dunkirk* and the *Great Western,* a publication showing that the GWR was justifiably proud of the work of its vessels, particularly in their participation at Dunkirk. Even the crewmen of the Dartmouth ferry *The Mew* were praised for their determination to take their tiny vessel into the war zone and become involved in rescuing troops, even although the crew and ship were eventually stood down. Similarly, GWR ships underwent great danger in approaching such French ports as St. Valery, La Pallice and Brest in 1940, in the hope of evacuating troops, often without naval escort. All this was described in some detail and with considerable pride (see Bibliography, under Brown).

In contrast, the LMS history by George C. Nash devotes only four pages to the work of the company's fleet, despite all but eight LMS ships being requisitioned at one time or another, and he refers to the 'fun' the crews had in the war. Little is made of the enormous sacrifices made by LMS ship crews, although the author does manage to list the number of decorations won by company seamen, no fewer than 27. One went to the Chief Officer on the *Duke of York* who picked up a live shell from the deck and threw it overboard. Fun indeed!

The Southern's war history *War on the Line* was well written by Bernard Darwin, and is probably the best of the four this author has examined. The sacrifices of the company's ships and crews are given deserved prominence; no less than 30% of the Southern's fleet was lost in the six years of war and the network underwent 170 enemy-caused 'incidents' per mile (the others were: GWR next, with 33 per mile, the LMS 29, LNER 28, according to Darwin), as well as the highest number

overall, nearly twice as many as the LMS. This author acknowledges his reliance on Mr. Darwin's book for a description of what D-Day was like for civilian ship crews taking part in the invasion; the reader of the Official History on the other hand will find it curiously lacking in detail, particularly relating to any part played by the railway ships. Away from the front, the Southern's marine workshops also 'did their bit'. At Dover Marine Works, requisitioned by the military from 1st July 1940 to the end of January 1945, the vessels of the Dover Patrol were maintained, while at the SR's Southampton workshops 957 ships were repaired, 184 of them warships, with another 774 (603 of them military) receiving attention at Newhaven.

The LNER's war history was the last of these four to appear, being published in the company's final year, 1947. Norman Crump's *By Rail to Victory* gives full attention to the Marine Division of the LNER, rightly emphasising the work of the paddle-steamers taken up as minesweepers, as well as the five former GCR and NER vessels working as rescue ships in the North Atlantic. The listing of the *Stockport* as 'missing' in this theatre after some four years is particularly poignant, with information about U-Boat strikes not then being fully available. On a more positive note, the LNER marine workshops at Harwich undertook £1 million-worth of repair work for both the Royal Navy and the Army, apparently on a contractual basis, although the Parkeston Quay complex had been taken over by the Navy in July 1940, as already mentioned. Mr. Crump went on to record that no fewer than 36 decorations had been awarded to the company's marine officers and men. His description of the loss of the *Amsterdam,* serving as a hospital ship after D-Day, is understated but is one of the most harrowing passages in any of the railway companies' histories.

Despite her wartime garb, the LNER's paddler Lucy Ashton *still operated as a civilian ship and is seen here on the Clyde in February 1945. An internal company memo records that in the second war – and she survived both – she carried nearly 900,000 passengers some 115,000 miles, missing only two days of scheduled service.*

When requisitioning civilian vessels in World War One, the Admiralty had warned commercial owners that they might not want their ships back once their military service was over. In practice, this proved to be true in only a few instances in 1919 and usually only if the vessel had been sunk and refloated, as in the case of the Great Eastern's *Brussels*. Additionally, there was a renewal of requisitions in 1918 and 1919 in order to tackle the legacy of mines, sown by both allied and enemy navies. These new commissions were being undertaken in peacetime, when the owners might have more opportunity to monitor the use of their vessels. But 1945 was different. The war had lasted two years longer than the first conflict, with enemy aircraft offering an additional danger to civilian ships.

Paddle steamers were among the first to find that the onset of peace would not necessarily reinvigorate their careers. Of 36 paddlers which survived the war (and not all of them had been requisitioned as minesweepers), 26 were able to resume service, including nine returning to railway ownership. Ten other surviving paddle steamers, five of them railway ships, were condemned as needing repairs or overhauls which could not be economically justified – for example, the *Eagle III* of the LMS required a renewed 'haystack' boiler which would have to be made specially and this did not happen. In any event, there was no swift renewal of a tourist industry after the war; no rail excursions were possible before 1948, cars could not be hired over more than a twenty-mile distance and there was a general air of austerity. The demand for trips 'round the bay' was obviously limited. Significantly, when the Southern decided to replace its lost paddle-steamers, it ordered turbine motor vessels – the *Brading, Southsea* and *Shanklin* entering service within a year of the company becoming part of British Railways.

One historic vessel which failed to make the transition back to railway service was the Great Western's tender, *Sir Walter Raleigh*. Like her 'sister' *Sir Francis Drake*, she was a veteran of two wars, the pair having been requisitioned before the end of July 1914, nearly a

After a glorious record of service in World War One, the Duchess of Argyll *undertook less martial duties in the second conflict, mainly tendering and ferrying in the Clyde. After nationalisation, she made her last civilian voyage in 1951 and was then bought by the Admiralty for experimental work in the Portland area.*

week before Britain declared war. *Sir Walter* was so extensively altered for military service in the second conflict, with her stern being cut away, that it was not considered worth refitting her and she was sold for breaking up in 1947. Nevertheless, this grand little ship was working as a tender at Cherbourg while in French ownership no less than twenty years later.

An LNER ship which came back from the dead, as it were, was the *St. Denis*. Sunk by scuttling after attack from the Luftwaffe off the Netherlands in May 1940, this former Great Eastern turbine vessel was raised by the Germans who employed her as a minesweeper. She was liberated by British troops in 1945, but leased to German users including Kiel University. In 1950 she was

taken to Sunderland under tow and then scrapped. Fellow Great Eastern ship *Malines* – she who 'sailed without orders' when expected to act as a sitting duck off Dunkirk – also returned to the UK after the war, but was unsuitable for further service. She had been beached after being attacked by aircraft off Alexandria on 22nd July 1942, but was then used for training purposes and was not listed by the Admiralty as a loss. Her tow back to the UK took nearly six months and she was sold for scrapping on arrival.

1945 was the last year of Total War to affect the United Kingdom. War in Europe ended on 8th May and in Asia on 15th August, but Britain had already decided to hold the General Election that was effectively postponed in 1940 – the last to be held had been five years earlier. Three weeks were needed to count the Services' votes in July 1945 and the results finally declared on the 26th showed that Labour had won a landslide victory which astonished even the new Prime Minister, Clement Attlee. From a transport point of view, this was going to mean nationalisation. The Labour Party was traditionally committed to nationalise 'the means of production, distribution and exchange' and a policy statement confirming this was issued in the first November of the new Parliament. Legislation followed in August 1947, with only the commercial road transport lobby putting up any major opposition, and a new British Transport Commission began sitting in that month. The new Transport Act established five executive bodies reporting to the new Commission, two of them already in existence. These were the Railway Executive and London Transport Executive, previously the London Passenger Transport Board. Joining them were the controversial Road Transport Executive and within six months similar bodies covering hotels and (together) docks and inland waterways .

Significantly, there was no Inshore or Coastal Shipping Executive, with British Railways now administering the fleets of the GWR, LMSR, LNER and SR, bringing more than 100 vessels under an authority which was regionalised to a major extent. The railways themselves were split into six Regions, all of which operated shipping, with the exception of the smallest, the North Eastern. Although it nominally held responsibility for Goole shipping, the Region did not operate this directly and railway connections with Scandinavia were organised from Liverpool Street, HQ of the Eastern Region.

While the pre-nationalisation companies had made some efforts to replace their vessels lost in the war, they might appear to have been slow to do so, although heavy yard occupation has to be taken into account, particularly with the need to replace mercantile ship losses. We have already seen that the LNER seemed to be having an internal debate about whether to replace its two lost Clyde steamers with one new vessel or two – the result of this discussion being the new, and present-day, *Waverley,* but their only other new ship was the

Arnhem, ordered from John Brown of Clydebank and commissioned for service on the Harwich station in May 1947. She was followed by the new *Amsterdam,* although in BR days. The company was keen to restore its train ferries as quickly as possible, particularly having lost Nos.2 and 3 of the pre-war vessels operating out of Harwich, to gunfire and mine respectively. The old No.1 was refitted, also by Brown's, to give a more conventional appearance with a single centred funnel, but she contributed another ten years' service while becoming worn out. She was joined by *Suffolk Ferry,* the company's first diesel-powered ship, and BR later added a sister vessel. In their history of nationalised shipping (see Bibliography) Messrs. Clegg and Styring make the enigmatic comment that "they have little to commend them in appearance though they can provide an interesting channel crossing for twelve passengers".

As mentioned earlier, the Southern ordered TSMVs to replace its Isle of Wight paddle ships, along with an DEPV for vehicular services. A sign of the times was the company's order for a new vehicle ferry for the Solent but, from the railway point of view, more relevant was the commissioning by the Southern of two new Channel 'packets'. These were the *Falaise* and a new *Maid of Orleans*.

The Great Western had lost two ships in World War Two, the *St. Patrick,* bombed as she made a scheduled passage across the Irish Sea in 1941, and the *St. David,* also bombed, but when serving as a hospital ship nearly three years later. A named replacement for the latter was ordered and delivered in 1947 shortly before the company was nationalised, and operated mainly on the Irish Sea route. The new *St. Patrick* was two months too late to work for the GWR and was to spend much of her career on Southern Region sailings. Despite this transfer, she sported the GWR crest on her bow, well into the 1960s.

The LMS had a number of replacement vessels to order, having lost such ferries as *Scotia* and *Princess Victoria*. The former was not actually replaced, the company instead deciding to order successors for the existing *Cambria* and *Hibernia*. These entered service within the first eighteen months of the new British Railways, their named predecessors, both having spent the war on domestic services, now making their last trip, to the scrapyard. *Princess Victoria* was replaced by a new ship of the same name and as close in design as to appear almost identical. Unfortunately, as mentioned

Having survived a war in which her sister Juno *was sunk by bombing, BR Scottish Region paddle steamer* Jupiter *is seen in the sunlit 1950s once more engaged in pleasure cruising. Known as* HMS Scawfell *during World War Two, she underwent another conversion, to oil fuelling, in 1956 but was then wastefully sold off within a year. This picture sums up the undying attraction of paddle steamers – vessels which 'did their bit' when called upon in war.*

---

earlier, the new 'Princess' sank in a severe storm in the North Channel in January 1953, with the loss of 133 lives. The name was never used again in BR service, future railway ships on this particular station being named *Caledonian Princess* and *Antrim Princess*.

If the private rail companies appeared slow to make good their wartime ships losses, the same could hardly be said for British Railways, which embarked on a positive programme of ship introduction from around 1950, particularly north of the Border. This dwarfed any reinvestment in the parent railway system it has to be said, and led, as economic historian T. R. Gourvish has pointed out, to the misleading impression that the

railways themselves were receiving a satisfactory level of investment, when in fact they were not.

The failure of the new Labour administration to establish an Inshore Shipping Executive was as disappointing as it was puzzling. The UK had no bridge or tunnel connections to any offshore island or to the Continent and ferries were obviously going to continue as an integral part of the commercial and passenger transport network for the foreseeable future (and still do). Yet this was a Government which believed that the near-moribund canal system was worthy of a state takeover – the growing recreational potential of inland waterways, if considered by transport planners at all, was not seen as a reason for nationalising them – but the nation's vitally-important ferries and cross-Channel steamers did not merit their own governing body. They were to continue, to a very large extent, to be run by railwaymen.

Lord Hurcomb, BTC Chairman, was quoted in the very first paragraph of this book as saying that ferries would continue as "a projection of the railway system across the narrow seas", yet he was prepared to see railway restaurant cars be administered by the Hotels Executive, and the railways were stripped of their involvement in bus and commercial road activities, with an immediate

Paddle steamer Caledonia *was the second railway vessel of that name. Plying for the LMS from 1934, her wartime service, as* HMS Goatfell, *began in the 11th minesweeping flotilla on the Clyde, before she was converted to an anti-aircraft role in 1942. She is seen here at Millport in happier days in 1966, three years before she left railway service.* (Mike Macdonald)

and damaging effect on their turnover. Curiously, Hurcomb had established his reputation as a 'safe pair of hands' in his administrative career with the Ministry of Shipping, yet he does not seem to have exuded enough personal influence to convince Whitehall, or indeed Westminster, of the need for a shipping executive. The 1947 Transport Act met this need halfway by establishing the CSAC, the Coastal Shipping Advisory Commission, and this included the leading officials of the new London Midland, Southern and Scottish Regions, even if no executive powers were held.

The omission of a shipping executive is made all the worse by the fact that railway ferries and Channel steamers were such a success! Even with the growth in air transport, travel needs have grown in proportion and the demand for inter-island and Continental travel is never-ending, although less so for pleasure cruising 'round the bay'. A separate Executive dealing with this would have been a boost for the concept of nationalised transport by associating state ownership with commercial success, something which hardly happened with railways. As it was, the railways lost their ships, which they were running so well, within twenty years. This eased in the privatisation process later introduced by governments of a rival hue and arguably accelerated the foreign takeover of Britain's shipping industry.

As mentioned in the first chapter, Britain's merchant navy proved too weak to provide all the ship tonnage required to back the Royal Navy Task Force in freeing the Falkland Islands from Argentina in 1982. Railway ships were now under the control of a semi-autonomous branch of British Rail trading under the name of Sealink, but were still some two years away from being sold off to commercial interests, as the political fashion of the time dictated. One railway ship which was called up was the *St. Edmund,* a BR ferry built at Birkenhead for the Harwich station in 1974. After a hasty eight-day conversion at Portsmouth, she sported a helipad in place of her after mast and set off southwards. Fortunately, peace was concluded by the time she had completed the 8,000-mile voyage, but that takes nothing away from her courageous crew, who would have heard about Exocet missiles being targeted on both naval and mercantile-origin craft with horrendous results. The Sealink ship was used to repatriate Argentine PoWs to the mainland and then as an accommodation ship at Port Stanley. On her return to the UK in 1983 she was purchased by the Ministry of Defence. Although spared the heat of war, the *St. Edmund* was nevertheless a worthy inheritor of a proud tradition.

In concluding the account of railway ships in World War One, this author commented that Field Marshal Haig was grateful to the South Eastern & Chatham Railway for its 'terrestrial' work, while seemingly unaware of the valour shown by its marine arm. As an army commander – and one who, unlike naval commanders, recognised the importance of the Railway Executive Committee – Haig was hardly in a position to be fully aware of the marine aspects of the company's (and other companies') efforts, but he showed his appreciation nevertheless. If on the other hand, one was to assess the contribution of the railway ships in Britain's war effort in World War Two by the official war history, *The War at Sea,* the reader would be tempted to conclude that naval vessels were the only ones worth mentioning on the world's oceans, with battleships and aircraft carriers well to the fore.

Without casting aspersions on her crew, this author would point out that the battlecruiser HMS *Repulse,* for example, scarcely fired a gun in anger while sailing in northern waters in World War Two, but is indexed 34 times in Captain Roskill's work, usually for joining or detaching from fleet formations. On the other hand, the railway steamer *Biarritz,* which was shelled and damaged off the French coast while helping to rescue the BEF during Operation Dynamo and took no fewer than 9,000 troops in fifteen trips to Normandy – where she was shelled again, is not mentioned at all. This book has attempted to be a small tribute to ships like the *Biarritz,* the *Maid of Orleans,* the *Roebuck, Princess Maud* and the *Waverley.* Some were sunk and the rest survived, only to be scrapped. We will not see their like again.

Like the Fair Maid *and the* Biarritz*, the* Lorina *of the LSWR appears to have been requisitioned in World War One even before her owners took possession of her. She served immediately as a troop transport. This happened again in the second conflict but she was unfortunately caught by the Luftwaffe at Dunkirk and sank in shallow water with eight crew lost.*

TABLES

Table I
The Railway Shipowners: Timeline

Pre-1922	1922	1923	1948
Caledonian		LMS	BR
Furness		LMS	BR
Glasgow & South Western		LMS	BR
Great Central		LNER	BR
Great Eastern		LNER	BR
Great Western		GWR	BR
Hull & Barnsley	To NER		
Lancashire & Yorkshire	To LNWR		
London & North Western		LMS	BR
London & South Western		SR	BR
London, Brighton & South Coast		SR	BR
Midland		LMS	BR
North British		LNER	BR
North Eastern		LNER	BR
South Eastern & Chatham		SR	BR

Table II
Railway Executive Committee Members 1916 in relation to War Office Liaison and RN requisitioning

Railway company	REC	Supplied RN	Secretary company To Army Command
Caledonian	*	*	
Great Central	*	*	
Great Eastern	*	*	
Great Northern	*	-	
Great Western	*	*	
Lancashire & Yorkshire	*	*	
London & North Western	*	*	Western
London & South Western	*	*	Southern
London, Brighton & South Coast	*	*	
Midland	*	*	
North Eastern	*	*	Northern
South Eastern & Chatham	*	*	Eastern
Furness	-	*	
Glasgow & South Western	-	*	
Great Northern of Ireland	-	-	Irish
North British	-	*	Scottish

Table III
Chronology of immediate railway ship requisition, to mid-August 1914
(Admiralty letters despatched to companies on 22nd July. War declared on 4th August)

End July	GWR	*Sir Francis Drake*	TSS	As: Tug
End July	GWR	*Sir Walter Raleigh*	TSS	Tug
8th August	LNWR	*Anglia*	TSS	Armed Boarder
8th August	LNWR	*Cambria*	TSS	Armed Boarder
8th August	LNWR	*Hibernia*	TSS	Armed Boarder
8th August	LNWR	*Scotia*	TSS	Armed Boarder
9th August	SECR	*Hythe*	TSS	Minesweeper
11th August	SECR	*Engadine*	TSS	Seaplane Carrier

Table IV
Redeployment of railway paddle-steamers following minesweeping, World War Two

Vessel	1st role	2nd	Remarks
Caledonia II (HMS *Goatfell*)	M/S	A.A. vessel	
Duchess of Fife	M/S	Training vessel	
Duchess of Rothesay	M/S	Accommodation ship	No further public service
Eagle III (HMS *Oriole*)	M/S	Accommodation ship	
Freshwater	Exam. vessel		
Jeanie Deans	M/S	A.A. vessel	
Juno (HMS *Helvellyn*)	M/S	A.A. vessel	Bombed during conversion
Jupiter (HMS *Scawfell*)	M/S	A.A. vessel	
Killingholme	Barrage balloon vessel		Requisitioned 1941
Kylemore	M/S	Netlayer	Lost, August 1940
Queen-Empress	M/S	A.A. vessel	
Ryde	M/S	A.A. vessel	Still in existence
Sandown	M/S	A.A. vessel	
Strathmore (HMS *Harlequin*)	Accom.ship		Wrecked 3.43
Talisman (HMS *Aristocrat*)	A.A. Vessel	HQ Ship, Normandy	
Whippingham	M/S	A.A. Vessel	Requisitioned 1941

Table V
Railway Ships Participating At Dunkirk, May/June 1940

All Southern Railway ships of more than 1,000 tons displacement and 150 miles range were requisitioned for Operation Dynamo on 29th May 1940, although these proved to be arbitrary parameters, and did not prevent the 1924 order of cargo vessels participating. The safest route to and from Dunkirk involved a return journey of 174 miles.

Autocarrier	Southern	
Biarritz	Southern	
Brighton Belle	Formerly Furness Railway	Lost 27th May
Brighton Queen	Formerly Furness Railway	Lost 31st May
Canterbury	Southern	
Cote d'Argent	Southern/French partners	
Cote d'Azur	Southern/French partners	
Dinard	Southern	
Duchess of Fife	LMS	
Eagle III (Oriole)	LMS	
Fishbourne	Southern	
Freshwater	Southern	Not officially listed as present at Dunkirk
Hythe II	Southern	
Isle of Guernsey	Southern	
Isle of Thanet	Southern	
King George V	Formerly LMS	
Lorina	Southern	Lost 29th May
Maid of Orleans	Southern	Withdrawn damaged after 31st May
Malines	LNER	
Manxman	Formerly LMS	
Marmion	LNER	
The Mew	GWR	Stood by
Newhaven	SR/SCNF	
Normannia	Southern	Lost 29th May
Oriole	See *Eagle III*	
Paris	Southern	Lost 2nd June
Prague	LNER	Damaged, beached Deal
Princess Maud	LMS	Damaged
Roebuck	GWR	
Rouen	Southern/SNCF	
St.Andrew	GWR	
St. David	GWR	
St. Helier	GWR	
St. Julien	GWR	
Sandown	Southern	
Scotia	LMS	Lost 1st June
Waverley	LNER	Lost 29th May
Whippingham	Southern	
Whitstable	Southern	
Wootton	Southern	Stood by
Worthing	Southern	Listed 'damaged' by Lloyds 2nd June

Table VI
Railway Ships Participating in Normandy landings (and aftermath), Summer 1944

Amsterdam	Hospital ship	Sunk by mine, 7th August
Biarritz	Troopship	Missed D-Day but was shelled during 15 trips
Canterbury	Troopship	
Dinard	Hospital ship	Mined, but survived
Duke of Argyll	Troopship	
Duke of Lancaster	Hospital ship	
Duke of Rothesay	Hospital ship	
Duke of Wellington (York)	Troopship	
Fratton	Examination Ship	Sunk, believed torpedoed
Hampton Ferry	Train Ferry	From August
Invicta	Troopship	
Isle of Guernsey	Troopship	
Isle of Jersey	Hospital ship	
Isle of Thanet	Troopship	
Maid of Orleans	Troopship	Torpedoed 28th June. (Originally believed mined)
Minster	Netlayer	Mined 8th June, Seine Bay
Prague	Hospital ship	
Princess Margaret	Troopship	
Princess Maud	Troopship	
Ringwood	Netlayer	
Ryde	A/A vessel	
St. Helier	Troopship	
St. Julien	Hospital ship	Mined, but survived
Talisman (HMS *Aristocrat*)	HQ ship	
Twickenham Ferry	Train Ferry	From August
Whippingham	A/A vessel	
Worthing (HMS *Brigadier*)	Troopship	

Some ships appear to have taken troops in and wounded out.

Table VII
Method of Railway Ship sinking, 1940-45

Year	Mined	Torp.	Bombed from air	Natural Cause	Other
1940					
	Mercury		Brighton		Ouse (collision?)
	Mersey		Kylemore		Train Ferry 2 (Gunf.)
	Princess Victoria		Maid of Kent		
			Lorina		
			Normannia		
			Paris		
			Scotia		
			Waverley		
			Bruges		
			St. Denis		
1941	Portsdown	Rye	Archangel		
	Southsea		Juno/Helvellyn		
			Marmion		
			St. Patrick		
			Tonbridge		
1942	St. Briac		Malines †		
1943		Stockport		Strathmore	
1944	Amsterdam	Fratton	St. David		
		Maid of Orleans			
	Minster				
1945	Daffodil				

† = Sunk but later refloated. *Malines* was torpedoed from the air.

FLEET LISTS   1914 and 1939

Some vessels will be found in more than one list, due to railway company takeovers, plus some served in both world wars.

• Source for Navy service dates : Colledge, Winser, (see bibliography) and individual company histories. Here is evidence of Admiralty service outside the dates published by Colledge, implying requisition for a short term and at short notice, as with, e.g. the LNWR's *Anglia*. Winser's work on WW2 ferries is admirably detailed. * Owned by associated company.

Caledonian Railway

Name	Type	Req?	When?	Discharged?	HMS?	Comments
*Caledonia**	PS	√	26.04.17	18.11.19		
*Duchess of Argyll**	TSS	√	11.02.15	27.04.19		
*Duchess of Fife**	PS	√	26.05.16	09.19	Duchess	
*Duchess of Hamilton**	PS	√	03.15			29.11.15 Mined. N. Sea
*Duchess of Montrose**	PS	√	15.05.15		Montrose	18.03.17 Mined. Channel
*Duchess of Rothesay**	PS	√	14.10.15	29.03.20	Duke of R.	
*Marchioness of Breadalbane**	PS	√	30.04.17	21.01.19		
*Marchioness of Lorne**	PS	√	19.06.16	09.19/20		Service as 1) Aux. Patrol vessel and 2)M/s

Marchioness of Bute left the fleet in 1908, but was involved in WW1.

Furness Railway

Name	Type	Req?	When	Discharged?	HMS?	Comments
Lady Evelyn	PS	√	4.17	6.19		Lost at Dunkirk 1940 (as *Brighton Belle*)
Lady Moyra	PS	√	21.11.15	9.7.19		Lost at Dunkirk 1940 (as *Brighton Queen*)

Glasgow & South Western

Name	Type	Req?	When	Discharged	HMS?	Comments
Atalanta	TrSS	√	3.12.15	26.6.19	Atalanta II	Also WW2
Glen Rosa	PS					
Glen Sannox I	PS	√	1914	1914		'Hired & returned'
Juno	PS	√	29.1.15	27.6.19	Junior	
Jupiter	PS	√	15.5.15	29.5.20		
Mars	PS	√	22.9.16		Marsa	Lost, collision 18.11.18
Mercury	PS	√	21.12.15	24.1.20		
Minerva	PS	√	19.6.16	7.4.20		2 periods of service
Neptune	PS	√	7.12.15		Nepaulin	Mined, 20.4.17
Troon	PS					Tug

Great Central

Name	Type	Req?	When?	Discharged?	HMS?	Comments
Accrington	SS	√	17.4.17	29.11.18		Also WW2
Brocklesby	PS	√	1916	1918		Fleet auxiliary
Bury	SS					Interned 1914
Central I	SS					Tug
Central II	SS					Tug
Chesterfield	SS	√	12.10.14			Sunk, Med. 18.5.18
City of Bradford	SS					Interned 1914

Great Central continued

Name	Type	Req?	When?	Discharged?	HMS?	Comments
City of Leeds	SS					Interned 1914
Cleethorpes	PS	√	19.9.16	19.4.19		
Dewsbury	SS					Also WW2
Immingham	SS	√	10.14			Lost, 6.6.15
Killingholme	PS	√	21.2.16	21.4.17		Also WW2
Leicester	SS	√	12.10.14			Mined, Folkestone, 12.2.16
Lutterworth	SS					
Macclesfield	SS					
Marple	TSS					Tender
Nottingham	SS					
Staveley	SS	√	10.14	7.16		
Stockport	SS					Lost in WW2
Wrexham	SS		11.16			Lost, 19.6.18

Great Eastern Railway

Name	Type	Req?	When?	Discharged?	HMS?	Comments
Amsterdam	TSS	√	31.10.14			
Antwerp				See *Roulers*		
Archangel	TrSS	√	7.5.15	19.4.19		Lost in WW2
Brussels	TSS					Sunk in German hands 1918, later sold
Clacton	TSS	√	7.10.14			Torpedoed 3.08.16
Colchester	TSS					Sunk in German hands, 2.3.18
Copenhagen	TrSS	√	12.10.14	12.16		Torpedoed 5.03.17
Cromer	TSS					
Dresden				See *Louvain*		
Kilkenny	SS					
Louvain	TSS	√	31.10.14			Torpedoed 21.1.18
Munich	TSS	√	12.10.14	then renamed *St.Denis* (qv)		
Newmarket	TSS	√	8.10.14			Torpedoed 16.7.16
Roulers	TSS	√	29.8.14	31.12.18		Also named *Antwerp & Vienna*
St. Denis	TrSS	√	7.10.15			Hospital ship. Scuttled/refloated WW2
St. Petersburg	TrSS	√	12.10.14	then see *Archangel*		
Stockholm	TSS	√	27.02.17	22.8.31	*Pegasus*	
Suffolk	PS	√				Naval tender
Vienna				See *Roulers*		

Great Western (1914-18)

Name	Type	Req?	When?	Discharged?	HMS?	Comments
Gazelle	TSS	√	27.10.14	4.20		
Great Western II	TSS					
Ibex	TSS					
Lynx	TSS	√	27.10.14	5.3.20	*Lynn*	
The Mew	TSS					Kingswear Ferry
Reindeer	TSS	√	2.10.14			Purchased, sold 1920
Roebuck	TSS	√	2.10.14		*Roedean*	Mined, 13.01.15
St. Andrew	TrSS					
St. David	TrSS					
St. Patrick	TrSS					
Sir Francis Drake	TSS	√	7.14	1.19		Tug, also in WW2
Sir Walter Raleigh	TSS	√	7.14	1.19		Tug, also in WW2

Lancashire & Yorkshire

Name	Type	Req	When?	Discharged?	HMS?	Comments
Aire	SS					
Alt	SS					WW2 service
Colleen Bawn	TSS					
Dearne	SS					Interned, lost in German hands, 12.12.15
Derwent	SS					
Don	SS	√	26.8.14			Lost 20.5.15
Duke of Albany	TSS	√	30.10.14			Torpedoed 26.8.16
Duke of Clarence	TSS	√	6.11.15	4.2.19		
Duke of Connaught	TSS					
Duke of Cornwall	TSS	√	31.10.14	1.2.19		
Hebble	SS	√	26.8.14			Mined 15.6.17
Hodder	SS	√	18.3.15	22.3.19		Also in WW2
Irwell	SS					
Mellifont	TSS					
Mersey	SS	√	17.9.14	6.17		Mined in WW2
Ouse	SS					Lost in WW2
Rother	SS					
Rye	SS					Torpedoed 7.4.18
Unity	SS					Torpedoed 2.5.18
Wharfe	SS					

London & North Western Railway

Name	Type	Req?	When?	Discharged?	HMS?	Comments
Anglia	TSS	√	8.8.14	5.15		Mined 16.11.15
Cambria	TSS	√	8.8.14			
Hibernia	TSS	√	8.8.14		Tara	Torp'd 5.11.15
Scotia II	TSS	√	8.8.14	1.8.17		Later, Menevia
Slieve Bloom	TSS					Sunk, collision, 3.18

London & South Western Railway
(Some ships owned jointly with LBSCR and also found in that company's list)

Name	Type	Req?	When?	Discharged	HMS?	Comments
Brittany	SS					
Duchess of Albany	PS					
Duchess of Fife	PS	√	23.3.16	9.12.19		
Duchess of Kent	PS	√	20.6.16	23.9.19		
Duchess of Norfolk	PS	√	17.5.16	19.4.19		Also in WW2
Duchess of Richmond	PS	√	17.5.16			Mined 28.6.19
Guernsey	SS					Wrecked 4.15
Hantonia	TSS					
Lorina	TSS					Lost in WW2
Normandy	SS					Tor. 25.1.18
Normannia	TSS					Lost in WW2
Princess Margaret	PS					
Sarnia	TrSS	√	14.11.14			Tor. Sept. 12th 1918
South Western	SS					Tor. 16.3.18

London, Brighton & South Coast Railway
(Some ships owned jointly with LSWR and also found in that company's list)

Name	Type	Req?	When?	Discharged?	HMS?	Comments
Anjou	TSS					Lost 1918
Arundel	TSS					
Bordeaux	TSS					
Brest	TSS					Lost 1917
Brighton	TrSS	√	29.6.15			Purchased 5.17 & sold on 4.19
Cherbourg	TSS					
Dieppe	TrSS					
Duchess of Albany	PS					
Duchess of Fife	PS	√	23.3.16	9.12.19		
Duchess of Kent	PS	√	20.6.16	23.9.19		
Duchess of Norfolk	PS	√	17.5.16	19.4.19		Also in WW2
Duchess of Richmond	PS	√	17.5.16			Mined, Aegean, 28.6.19
France	TSS					
Maine	TSS					Tor. 1917
Newhaven	TrSS					
Paris	TSS	√	14.11.4	4.19		Sunk at Dunkirk in WW2
Portsmouth	TSS					
Princess Margaret	PS					
Rouen	TrSS					
Sussex	TSS					French-owned after damage, 1916

Midland Railway

Name	Type	Req?	When?	Discharged?	HMS?	Comments
Antrim	TSS					
City of Belfast	TSS	√	30.10.14	3.10.19		
Donegal	TSS	√	Not known			Tor. 17.04.17
Duchess of Devonshire	TSS	√	30.10.14	6.11.19		
Londonderry	TrSS					
Manxman	TrSS	√	4.16			Purchased, seaplane carrier
Wyvern	TSS	√	15.3.15	1919		Tug, renamed Wickstead

North British Railway

Name	Type	Req?	When?	Discharged?	HMS?	Comments
Dandy Dinmont	PS					
Duchess of Buccleuch	PS	√	12.7.16			Then bought by Adm. Sold 1923
Edinburgh Castle*	PS	√	19.7.16			Destroyed, Murmansk, 24.9.19
Empress*	PS	√	1919			For 2 weeks only
Fair Maid	PS	√	12.7.15			Mined, North Sea, 9.11.
Kenilworth	PS					
Lady Clare	PS	√	25.5.17	24.12.18		
Lady Rowena	PS	√	12.4.16	6.2.19		Two service periods when non-railway
Lord Morton*	PS	√	4.18			Destroyed, White Sea 1919
Lucy Ashton	PS					
Marmion	PS	√	15.5.15	27.5.20		Lost in WW2
Redgauntlet*	PS	√	4.6.16	30.7.17		Bought by Adm. Sold 1919
Talisman I	PS	√	6.17	10.19	Talla	
Waverley III	PS	√	15.9.15	9.7.20		Lost in WW2
William Muir	PS	√	7.6.17	21.5.19		

Stirling Castle left fleet in 1907 and was lost minesweeping in 1916. * Owned by associated company

North Eastern Railway

Name	Type	Req?	When?	Discharged?	HMS?	Comments
Cito	SS					Sunk by destroyer, 17.5.17
Darlington	SS					
Harrogate	SS					Foundered 20.2.18
Hero	SS					
Hull	SS					Sold commercially 4.15
Jervaulx Abbey*	SS					
Juno	SS					Damaged by enemy action 19.10.17
Kirkham Abbey*	SS					Torpedoed 27.7.18
Lord Joicey	SS					Dredger, hired by GCR
Otto	SS					
Rievaulx Abbey*	SS					Mined 3.9.16
Truro	SS					Sunk by sub. 7.5.15
Whitby Abbey	SS	√	10.12.15	23.12.19		
York	SS	√	3.1.15	4.4.19		

South Eastern & Chatham Railway

Name	Type	Req?	When?	Discharged?	HMS?	Comments
Achille Adam	TSS					Tor. 23.3.17
Biarritz	TSS	√	2.15	1919		Also in WW2
Empress	TrSS	√	25.8.14	11.19		Seaplane carrier
Engadine	TrSS	√	11.8.14	12.19		Seaplane carrier, at Jutland
Folkestone	TSS	√	9.10.14	31.1.20		
Hythe	TSS	√	10.14			Sunk after collision 28.10.15
Invicta	TrSS					
Maid of Orleans	TSS					
Maidstone	SS					
Onward	TrSS					Scuttled 1918 & refloated
The Queen	TrSS					
Riviera	TrSS	√	11.8.14	31.5.19		Also in WW2 as Laird's Isle
Victoria	TrSS					

Great Western (1939-45)

Name	Type	Req?	When?	Discharged?	HMS?	Comments
Great Western III	TSS	√	4.44.	8.44		
The Mew	TSS					Kingswear Ferry.. Stood by for Dunkirk service
Roebuck II	TSS	√	22.10.40	10.10.45		Renamed *Roebuck II* in 1942
St. Andrew II	TSS	√	11.9.39	8.46		
St. David II	TSS	√	25.9.39			Sunk at Anzio
St. Helier	TSS	√	5.40	8.45		
St. Julien	TSS	√	9.9.39	1.46		
St. Patrick II	TSS	√	9.39	10.39		Sunk on company service 6.41
Sambur	TSS	√	10.40	6.45	*Toreador*	
Sir Francis Drake	TSS	√	25.8.39	1946		
Sir John Hawkins	TSS	√	1.41	10.45		
Sir Richard Grenville II	TSS	√	8.39	1.46		
Sir Walter Raleigh	TSS	√	8.39	8.46		

London Midland & Scottish Railway

Name	Type	Req?	When?	Discharged?	HMS?	Comments
Aire II*	SS		8.40	9.45		
Alt*	SS	√	.40	.45		Not continuous service
Anglia	TSS					
Arran Mail	TSMV					
Caledonia II*	PS	√	.39	.45	Goatfell	
Cambria	TSS					
Countess of Breadalbane*	TSMV					
Dearne*	SS	√				Refrigerated meat carri
Don*	SS					
Duchess of Fife*	PS	√	11.39	1.45		
Duchess of Hamilton*	TrSS					
Duchess of Montrose*	TrSS	√				
Duchess of Rothesay*	PS	√	11.39	.45		Condemned 1946
Duke of Argyll	TSS	√	9.39	6.45		Not continuous service
Duke of Lancaster	TSS	√	1.44	12.45		
Duke of Rothesay	TSS	√	9.43	.46		
Duke of York	TSS	√	9.39	11.46	Duke of Wellington	
Eagle III *	PS	√	11.39	8.45		Condemned 1946
Fair Maid	PS	√	.40	.45		Condemned 1945
Glen Sannox II*	TrSS					
Hibernia	TSS					
Hodder*	SS					
Irwell	SS	√	8.43	. 46		
Isle of Skye*	PS		12.40	.45		
Juno*	PS	√	10.39		Helvellyn	Bombed 20.3.41
Jupiter	PS	√	10.39	.45	Scawfell	
King Edward*	TSS	√	1.45	. 46		
Kylemore*	PS	√	9.39			Sunk 21.8.40
Marchioness of Graham	TSS					
Marchioness of Lorne II*	PS					
Mercury II*	PS	√	9.39			Sunk 25.12.40
Mersey*	SS					
Ouse*	SS	√	6.40	6.40		Sunk 8.8.40
Princess Margaret	TSS	√	1.44	10.44		
Princess Maud	TSS	√	9.39	9.45		Damaged at Dunkirk
Princess Victoria	TSMV	√	9.39			Mined 18.5.40
Queen-Empress*	PS	√	10.39	.44		
Rother*	SS					
Rye*	SS					Torpedoed 7.3.41 24 killed
Scotia III	TSS	√	12.39			Bombed & sunk, 1.6.40
Slieve Bawn II	TSS					
Slieve Bearnagh	TSS					
Slieve Donard	TSS					
Slieve League	TSS					
Slieve More II	TSS					
Strathmore*	PS	√	9.42		Harlequin	Wrecked 3.43
Wee Cumbrae *	TSMV					

London & North Eastern Railway

Name	Type	Req?	When?	Discharged?	HMS?	Comments
Accrington	SS	√	2.42	3.46		
Amsterdam	TSS	√	9.39			Mined 7.8.44
Antwerp	TSS	√	.39			
Archangel	TrSS	√	12.39			Lost 16.5.41

London & North Eastern Railway continued

Name	Type	Req?	When?	Discharged?	HMS?	Comments
Bruges	TSS	√	9.39			Lost, 12.6.40
Bury	SS	√	4.41	6.46		Also, intended blockship 9.39
Dewsbury	SS	√	7.41	8.45		
Felixstowe	SS	√	6.40	1.46	*Colchester*	
Jeanie Deans	PS	√	10.39	.44		
Lucy Ashton	PS					
Macclesfield	SS					
Malines	TSS	√	4.40			Torpedoed 7.42 but refloated & sold
Marmion	PS	√	10.39			Bombed 9.4.41
*Melrose Abbey**	SS	√	3.41	6.45		
Prague	TSS	√	12.39	6.45		Damaged at Dunkirk
St. Denis	TrSS	√				Scuttled 5.40, raised by Germans
Sheringham	SS	√	6.40	3.46		Min. War Transport use
Stockport	SS	√	7.41			Lost 2.43
Talisman	PS	√	10.39	.46	*Aristocrat*	
Train Ferry No.1	TSS	√	9.39	5.46	*Princess Iris*	
Train Ferry No.2	TSS	√	6.40			Lost 12.6.40
Train Ferry No.3	TSS	√	6.40		*Daffodil*	Mined 17.3.45
Vienna	TSS	√	6.41			Then purchased for MoWT service
Waverley	PS	√	10.39			Bombed & Sunk 29.5.40

Southern Railway

Name	Type	Req?	When?	Discharged?	HMS?	Comments
Autocarrier	TSS	√	5.40	.45		
Biarritz	TSS	√	9.39			Retained
Brighton	TSS	√	5.40	5.40		Bombed and sunk 24.5.40
Brittany	TSS	√	29.5.40	.45		Served in Indian Ocean
Canterbury	TSS	√	5.40	1.46		
Deal	TSS	√	5.41	10.43		
Dinard	TSS	√	10.39	.46		Damaged, D-Day+1
Fishbourne	DTSMV					
Fratton	TSS	√	8.40			Lost, 18.8.44
Freshwater	PS					
Hampton Ferry	TSS	√	9.39	.46	*Hampton Minelayer*, then MWT ferry 7.40-.46	
Hantonia	TSS	√	4.42	7.45		
Haslemere	TSS	√	10.41	.45		Balloon barrage ship
Hythe	TSS	√	5.40	6.45		
Invicta II	TSS	√	4.42	.46		
Isle of Guernsey	TSS	√	8.40	.45		
Isle of Jersey	TSS	√	8.39	.45		
Isle of Sark	TSS	√	12.41	6.46		Radar training
Isle of Thanet	TSS	√	9.39	.45		
Lorina	TSS	√	9.39			Sunk at Dunkirk
Lymington	TSMV					
Maid of Kent	TSS	√				Lost 5.40
Maid of Orleans	TSS	√	9.39			Damaged at Dunkirk. Torpedoed after D-Day
Maidstone	TSS	√	6.40	6.45	*Bungay*	
Merstone	PS					
Minster	TSS	√	29.8.40			Mined Normandy 8.6.44
Normannia	TSS	√	5.40			Sunk at Dunkirk
Paris	TSS	√	9.39			Sunk at Dunkirk
Portsdown	PS					Mined 20.9.41
Ringwood	TSS	√	9.41	6.46		

Southern Railway continued

Name	Type	Req?	When?		Comments
Ryde	PS	√	27.2.40	.47	
St. Briac	TSS	√	7.6.41		Mined 12.3.42
Sandown	PS	√	10.39	.46	
Shepperton Ferry	TSS	√	8.39	2.46	*Shepperton*
Southsea	PS	√	2.40		Mined 16.2.41
Tonbridge	TSS	√	10.40		Bombed & Sunk 22.8.41
Twickenham Ferry	TSS	√	6.40	7.46	
Whippingham	PS	√	.41	4.46	
Whitstable	TSS	√	5.40	5.45	
Wootton	DTSMV				
Worthing	TSS	√	.39	3.45	*Brigadier*

All SR ships of more than 1,000 tons displacement and 150 miles range were requisitioned for Operation Dynamo on 29th May 1940, although these proved to be arbitrary parameters and did not prevent the 1924 order of cargo vessels participating.

British Rail (Sealink)

Name	Type	Req?	When?	Comments
St. Edmund	TSMV	√	4.82	Sent to Falklands, purchased by MoD on return

Abbreviations
AMC - Armed Merchant Cruiser
GM – General Manager
DEMV – Diesel Electric Motor Vessel
HMHS - His/Her Majesty's Hospital Ship
HMS - His/Her Majesty's Ship
LC - Landing Craft
LCI (H) – Landing Craft Infantry (with hand-operated davits)
LCT - Landing Craft Tank
LSI – Landing Ship Infantry
MV - Motor Vessel
PS - Paddle Steamer
QSTS - Quadruple Screw Turbine Steamer
QSTES - Quadruple Screw Turbo-Electric Steamer
RE – Railway Executive 1939-52
REC – Railway Executive Committee, 1914-20
RFA - Royal Fleet Auxiliary
RMS - Royal Mail Ship/Steamer
SP - Steam Packet
SS - Steam Ship
ST - Steam Tug
SV - Sailing Vessel
TS – Turbine
TSMV – Turbine Screw Motor Vessel
TSS - Triple/Turbine Screw Steamer
TES - Turbo-Electric Steamer

Bibliography

Archives

BR/CSP/1/3 (NAS) Caledonian Steam Packet Company, Board Minutes 1914-19.

BR/LNE/8/376 and 383 Ministry of Shipping correspondence on requisition 1940. Latter file includes script for BBC radio programme on paddle steamers in WW2 by W.R. Orr, based on interviews in 1946.

BR/REC(S)/1/1,22, and 25 Railway Executive Committee circulars, 1914-5, as received by GNR and NBR.

Lloyd's War Losses: The First World War. Casualties to Shipping through Enemy Causes, 1914-1918. [MS facsimile]. Lloyds of London Press, 1990.

Lloyd's War Losses: *The Second World War. Casualties to Shipping through Enemy Causes, 1939-1945.* [MS facsimile in 2 v]. Lloyds of London Press, 1990-1.

Books

British Vessels lost at sea, 1914-18 and 1939-45. 3rd edn. PSL reprint, 1988.

Brown, A. *Dunkirk and the Great Western.* GWR, 1945.

Clegg, W.P. and Styring, J.S. *British Nationalised Shipping, 1947-1968.* New York, Kelley, 1969.

Colledge, J.J. *Ships of the Royal Navy.* 2v. Greenhill, 1987.

Corbett, J.S. and Newbolt, H. *Naval Operations [in the Great War].* Vols.1-5. Longmans, 1920-31.

Credland, Arthur G. *The Wilson Line.* Tempus, 2000.

Crump, N. *By Rail to Victory: the story of the LNER in wartime.* 1947.

Darwin, B. *War on the Line: the story of the Southern Railway in wartime.* 1946.

Divine, A.D. *Behind the Fleets.* John Murray, 1940.

Divine, A.D. *The Nine Days of Dunkirk.* Pan, 1964.

Dow, G. *Great Central. Vol.3.* Ian Allan, 1965.

Duckworth, C.L.D. and Langmuir, G.E. *Clyde River and other steamers.* 3rd edn. 1972.

Duckworth, C.L.D. and Langmuir, G.E. *Railway and other steamers.* Glasgow, 1948.

Edwards, B. *The Grey Widow-Maker.* Futura, 1995.

Gilbert, Sir Martin. *First World War.* HarperCollins, 1995.

Greenway, Ambrose. *A century of North Sea passenger steamers.* Ian Allan, 1986.

Hocking, C. *Dictionary of Disasters at Sea during the Age of Steam 1824-1962.* 2v. Lloyds, 1969.

Hough, Richard. *The Great War at Sea, 1914-1918.* OUP, 1983.

Jones, J.H. *Josiah Stamp, public servant*, Pitman, 1964.

King, P. *The Channel Islands at War, 1940-1945.* Hale, 1991.

Lavery, Brian. *Shield of Empire.* Birlinn, 2007.

Nash, G.C. *The LMS at War.* LMS, 1946.

North Eastern Railway Association. *North Eastern Record,* Vol. 1., 1988.

Plummer, R. *Paddle Steamers at War, 1939-45.* Peterborough, 1995.

Plummer, R. *The Ships that saved an Army.* PSL, 1990.

Pratt, E.A. *British railways and the Great War.* 2v. Selwyn & Blount, 1921.

Reynolds, D. *In command of history.* Allen Lane, 2004.

Roskill, S.W. *The War at Sea 1939-1945.* 3v. HMSO, 1954.

Taylor, A.J.P. *War by timetable: how the First World War began.* Macdonald, 1969.

Winser, J.d.S. *Short sea: long war: cross-Channel ships' naval and military service in World War II.* World Ship Society, 1997.

References in the text to Mass Observation are based on edited extracts by Simon Garfield in his books *We are at War* and *Private Battles* (Ebury Press, 2005 and 2006 respectively) - invaluable and sometimes astonishing sources of historical information.

Acknowledgments

Permission to reproduce material from A.D. Divine's 1940 work *Behind the Fleets* was received courtesy of John Murray Publishing. Michael Joyce, now recently deceased, kindly provided recollections of escorting work on destroyers. My thanks also go to Mike Macdonald for patiently reading early drafts of this work, and for his constructive comments, and to Geoffrey Hughes and Richard Lacey for information. I would particularly like to thank Campbell MacCutcheon for picture researching and Jerzy Swieszkowski for information on Great Eastern operations in WW1. I acknowledge the helpful assistance rendered by the staffs of the National Archives of Scotland, National Library, and Edinburgh City Libraries, Aberdeen Art Gallery, and the Anglesey Record Office. Finally, thanks are due to Michael Blakemore and Barry C. Lane for their editorial and design work on this book.

INDEX OF SHIPS

(Some non-railway and RN warships included)

125